C000176489

Gho
of
Berkshire

Ian McLoughlin

*To my old mate Linda .....
with whom I have spent many
very happly hours .... I love you
dearly ...*   *[signature]*

COUNTRYSIDE BOOKS
NEWBURY, BERKSHIRE

First Published 1995
© Ian McLoughlin 1995

All rights reserved.
No reproduction permitted
without the prior permission
of the publishers:

Countryside Books
3 Catherine Road
Newbury, Berkshire

ISBN 1 85306 265 0

Dedicated to all the hard-working librarians in the Royal County of Berkshire, without whose unstinting help this book would not have been possible.

Cover illustration by Colin Doggett

Produced through MRM Associates Ltd., Reading
Typeset by Textype Typesetters, Cambridge
Printed by J. W. Arrowsmith Ltd., Bristol

Contents

Great
Shefford

Pangbourne

Bucklebury

Kintbury   Thatcham   Woolhampto

NEWBURY   Brimpton

Crookham
Common

Bisham
Abbey
Hurley
MAIDENHEAD
SLOUGH
Wargrave
Eton
WINDSOR
Datchet
Windsor
Forest
READING
eale
BRACKNELL
ley

Foreword

THE Royal County of Berkshire is teeming with ghosts; but few of them seem to do very much. Grey Ladies walk on dark nights everywhere – but why? No one knows. This book is an attempt to find out why our county's ghosts come back to haunt us; to find the tragic story behind the spirit's need to walk abroad.

Many of the ghosts in these pages led turbulent lives, and it seems they could not rest easy in their graves without leaving the imprint of their souls on the world of the living. Research into their lives gives us lots of clues why their spirits are unquiet, and much historical detail is necessarily recorded here.

Most of us are uncommitted when asked if we believe in ghosts. But during the course of writing this book, I have often felt as if someone was watching over my shoulder, a sort of unseen censor from another world. On two separate occasions, my trusty word processor, hitherto completely reliable, went completely haywire. On both occasions the repair technician was absolutely nonplussed, and found nothing wrong with the machine. But in my thoughts, I fancy I can hear the faint echo of ghostly laughter. They have had the last word.

Ian McLoughlin
Autumn 1995

1

The Baleful Ghost of Lady Hoby

BISHAM Abbey is a beautiful old manor house on the banks of the Thames between Henley and Maidenhead. Bisham is a typical English riverside village, with wild flowers in the water meadows; and the May trees bloom in springtime beside the peaceful river. But when the sun goes down, the abbey's history comes back to haunt it. The history of Bisham Abbey is as complicated as it is blood-curdling. In earlier times, most of the owners were murdered, killed in battle or executed for treason.

But the abbey is haunted not by one of these distressed souls, robbed of their lives at the whim of others, but by one of the most remarkable and successful women in English history. Her name was Dame Elizabeth Hoby, and she was a personal friend and close confidante of Elizabeth I.

Despite its name, Bisham Abbey was never a religious institution, although the village did at one time have an Augustinian priory. At the time of the Domesday survey in 1086, the Manor of Bisham belonged to Henry de Ferrers. His grandson granted it to the Knights Templar, who were abolished by Edward II in 1307 when the estate became the property of Roger de Winkfield. The oldest parts of the house, including the Great Hall, date back to the Templars.

The overlording remained with the Ferrers family until 1266, when it was granted to the Earl of Lancaster. In 1322, Thomas, Earl of Lancaster was executed at Pontefract in Yorkshire, and Bisham passed to Hugh le Despenser. He was beheaded in 1326 and the manor reverted to the Crown. Later it was given to William, Lord Montague, who was made

Earl of Salisbury in 1337. It was his son who set up the Augustinian priory, which was seized by Henry VIII when he dissolved the Roman Catholic church in England. The last abbot of Bisham left a curse on any family which dared to live there. Plenty of blood had already been spilled, and there was a lot more to come.

Lordship passed from the Montague family to Richard Neville, who was beheaded, also at Pontefract, after the battle of Wakefield in 1460.

Bisham became the property of Edward, Earl of Warwick, but he was beheaded in 1499 for attempting to escape from the Tower of London. His father, the Earl of Clarence, was drowned in a butt of Malmsey wine. In 1523, Henry VIII granted the manor to Clarence's daughter, Lady Margaret, wife of Sir Richard Pole, and created her Countess of Salisbury. Henry described her as 'the most saintly woman in England', and she was for many years highly favoured at court. But the family's bad luck caught up with her when her son Reginald, Archbishop of Canterbury, denounced the king's ecclesiastical policy.

Because the archbishop had fled out of Henry's reach, the king arrested all the other members of the family. The countess was locked in the Tower of London for two years and then executed. Her great grandfather had been beheaded, her grandfather, Richard, Earl of Warwick, hanged at Barnet, her father murdered by his brother, Edward IV, and her brother executed on Tower Hill by Henry VII. She was laid to rest in the Tower Chapel.

The king, having got rid of the old lady in the inevitably ruthless manner he employed with anybody who disagreed with him, conferred the manor on his discarded German wife, Anne of Cleves. She never took up residence, and in 1552, after Henry's death, she was ordered by Edward VI to exchange the property so that Edward could grant Bisham to Sir Philip Hoby, a rising star in the diplomatic world.

Hoby found the manor in considerable decay, and immediately set about restoring it. He died in 1558, and was succeeded by his half-brother Thomas, who continued with the restoration work. A family tomb was established, and the mutilated remains of many of the previous owners were buried there. Their graves lie under what are now the lawns and tennis courts to the north east of the house.

Sir Thomas Hoby followed in the footsteps of his distinguished elder brother. He was a graduate of St John's College, Cambridge, and was a very learned man. Like Sir Philip, he served in the diplomatic corps, spoke several languages and had travelled widely. He was ambassador to the French court when he died, and his body was brought back to Bisham to be buried. Eight years later his widow Elizabeth married Lord John Russell, Earl of Bedford, whom she also outlived. She had borne three children by her first husband, and had three more by her second. She had a special chapel constructed in the parish church of All Saints in memory of the two men, with a fine display of heraldry and their recumbent effigies on the altar-stone. Next to it, she set up an even more splendid tomb for herself. She is shown kneeling beneath a canopy, surrounded by her children.

Dame Elizabeth was the daughter of Sir Anthony Cooke of Gidea Hall in Essex. Her family enjoyed a high reputation for scholarship and she herself was a remarkable woman, conversant in Latin, Greek and French. She busied herself with scholarly work, and translated from the French a learned work on the Eucharist. She seems to have had a macabre obsession with funereal pomp and splendour, and indulged herself burying two husbands and four children, all of whom died prematurely. She made elaborate arrangements for her own funeral, and a letter survives from her to the Garter-King-of-Arms, in which she inquires how many mourners she could have, how many pages, gentlemen ushers, chief mourners, lords and gentlemen, the manner of her hearse, of the heralds and the church.

Dame Elizabeth died on 2nd June 1609 at the age of 81. Her ghost walks at Bisham, like Lady Macbeth, perpetually washing her hands, to atone for the murder of one of her sons. He was not a good scholar, and when he splattered his writing book with ink blots Lady Hoby flew into a rage and beat him senseless. Then she locked him in a tiny closet and left him. A summons came for her to come urgently to her friend, the queen, who enjoyed spending time at Bisham. When she returned to the closet the boy was dead. Builders working on the house in 1860 found the room, which had been sealed up. In it was a 16th-century copy book covered in ink stains.

The son is thought to be Thomas, her younger son by her first marriage, and not his mother's favourite. She referred to him as a 'scurvy urchin' and a 'spindle shanked ape'. He was certainly a bad lot, and even though only a boy, he was soon in trouble with the authorities. An account of Star Chamber proceedings describes him as 'ye busyest sawcie little Jackie in all the countrie'.

Dame Elizabeth's full-length portrait still hangs in the Great Hall at Bisham, and when the mood takes her, her wraith glides down off the wall to terrorise all and sundry. The last family to own Bisham were the Vansittarts. One evening, Admiral E.H. Vansittart and his brother had been playing chess. The admiral was the last to retire to bed, and was standing in the Great Hall where Lady Hoby's portrait hangs. There was not a sound or movement in the room, but Admiral Vansittart was suddenly aware of someone standing behind him. He turned to see the ghost of Lady Hoby in her black dress and Elizabethan bonnet. He turned to where her portrait hung on the oak-panelled wall. The frame was empty.

Dame Elizabeth's ghost has terrorised many a visitor to Bisham, and house guests of the Vansittart family were often badly frightened. Those bold enough to look at her portrait in the hall would sometimes find her standing next to them.

One guest at the house awoke in terror in the middle of the night. He could hear water dripping in his bedroom, and the gun dog that was with him was whining with fright. The drip, drip, drip got louder and louder, and nearer and nearer, but he could see nothing in the pitch black. Man and dog were rooted to the spot. When the water seemed to be dripping onto the carpet right beside the dog, it made a terrified leap onto the bed, landing on top of his master, who promptly fainted. When he woke up, it was morning. The sun was shining through the curtains, the dog was curled up fast asleep, and close inspection of the carpet showed it to be as dry as a bone.

Another guest to feel the sharp animosity of Lady Hoby was a young woman in Victorian times who was visiting from London with a party of house guests. Tired from the journey, she retired to her room early and left her companions chatting downstairs.

Some little while later, she came running downstairs, screaming hysterically. With tears streaming down her cheeks, she pointed wildly up the staircase and sobbed breathlessly that she had been attacked by an old woman dressed in black. The other guests settled her down and she was brought smelling salts and brandy. The braver souls in the party ventured warily up to her room.

There they found her belongings strewn all over the floor. Her bedside clock had been hurled into the fireplace and was smashed to pieces. All the items on her dressing table had been swept aside, and were scattered around the room. Her elegant hairbrushes were ruined from being thrown against the wall, and make-up and perfume were spilled over the bed. No one had heard a thing.

A similar incident was experienced by another young woman who came to the abbey for a weekend party and dance during the First World War. She also retired early, and was comfortably tucked up in her four poster bed, with her West Highland terrier beside her. She was drowsing and reading a book when unseen hands suddenly ripped down the bed-curtains. Again, all the items on the dressing table were swept onto the floor. Her diamond watch was hurled into the far corner. A pile of sheet-music was lifted out of its case and scattered round the room. The dog fled, howling in terror.

Then the young lady saw the outline of a figure. The shape grew stronger, and she perceived a tall woman, wearing a black dress, standing next to the bed, haughty and aloof, with thin and cruel features. Then she vanished.

It took some time for the distraught victim to calm down enough to relate her terrible experience. The other people in the house did their best to reassure her, and after a while, they asked her if she could describe the apparition. The girl walked straight to Lady Hoby's portrait and pointed unflinchingly at it.

The ghostly dame must have taken a severe dislike to these two hapless young women. Most of her manifestations show her icy calm and implacable authority.

Her chill malevolence was demonstrated one night when a young man settled down to sleep on a couch in the library. He was a rowing blue, and was competing at Henley Regatta. He was a good-looking young man, and very vain, with a handsome head of hair of which he was inordinately proud.

He woke up in a cold sweat to find the ghost of Lady Hoby standing next to him. He was terrified, but worse was to come. The ghostly apparition leaned over him and motioned with a bony finger towards his golden tresses. 'Young man,' said Lady Hoby, 'if I but touch thee, thou wilt be bald.' He ran screaming from the house and joined a monastery, a sad loss to the rowing fraternity.

Dame Elizabeth also haunts the lane leading to the main road, and has been seen in a boat on the river. Some young boys out on a late fishing trip ran for their lives when they saw her, dressed all in black, in a ghostly boat near the abbey.

Bisham remained in the Hoby family until 1780, when it was sold to George Vansittart, who had made his fortune out in India. On the death of his grandson in 1885, Bisham passed to his cousin, Edward Vansittart-Neale. He was a remarkable man and a successful barrister, but became interested in the Co-operative movement and moved to Manchester. Whenever the society needed money, he sold off bits of Bisham land. He became the first general secretary of the Co-operative Society and was known as its 'Father'. A monument was erected to him in St Paul's Cathedral.

During both World Wars, the abbey was used as a hospital. A nurse on night duty in 1944 was attending to a patient when she heard the loud sobbing of someone obviously in distress. She went to find out what the matter was, but found all her patients calm and sleeping. She concluded that the ghostly weeping was not of this world. She was one of many people who have heard the mysterious crying. Some have seen the figure of a woman in Elizabethan dress perpetually washing her hands as she glides through the house, preceded by a small bowl which moves before her.

After the war, Miss Phyllis Vansittart-Neale offered the abbey as a memorial to her two nephews, both victims of the conflict, and it was sold to the Central Council of Physical Recreation to perpetuate the use of the place for the youth of England.

When Henry VIII took Bisham for himself, the abbot left a curse. He declared that any family which lived at the abbey would see its sons come to a bloody end. The curse certainly proved true over the ages, and many of the Vansittart family met untimely deaths, with sons dying in infancy and young men lost in battle. Perhaps the abbot foresaw the murder of Thomas by his mother, and condemned her to haunt the house forever, washing her hands for eternity.

2

Lady Bolingbroke of Bucklebury

THE restless spirit of the Lady of the Manor still haunts the village of Bucklebury on dark and stormy nights.

Lady Bolingbroke's marriage was not a happy one, and she died of a broken heart soon after being deserted by her husband in the early 18th century. Her ghost has been seen, crying bitterly, as she rides through the village in a ghostly carriage pulled by six black horses, accompanied by a headless postillion.

She was born Frances Winchcombe, the last in the line of the famous Jack O'Newbury family whose history has been researched by Newbury author and historian Cecilia Millson. She tells how Frances was devastated when her husband was forced to flee the country.

'Bolingbroke was accused of taking part in a Jacobite plot against the government. He was forced to flee the country under threat of impeachment and his wife never saw him again.'

Bolingbroke was born Henry St John and married Frances in 1701. Her father, also Henry, died in 1703, and Bucklebury Manor was inherited by his daughter and son-in-law. The manor was originally owned by the Abbot of Reading, who had an abundance of property throughout the county. At the dissolution of the monasteries by Henry VIII in 1536, the king granted the manor to John Winchcombe, the son of Jack O'Newbury. It was common practice for monks to construct fish ponds to ensure a ready supply of year round fresh food. Legend has it that the ghosts of the monks haunt the area around the ponds, which are still in use in the grounds of Bucklebury Manor.

For a while, Henry and Frances were very happy. They entertained lavishly at the manor, and many of the famous literary figures of the day came to visit them, including Jonathan Swift, author of *Gulliver's Travels*, John Gay, Alexander Pope, who lived nearby at Ufton Court, and many others.

Henry St John was created Viscount Bolingbroke in 1712. By this time, the marriage was in a sorry state. He finally deserted Frances in 1715, after slipping away through a secret tunnel at the manor and taking ship from Dover to escape his pursuers.

Frances was broken hearted, and still very much in love with him – she would not hear a word said against him. She died in 1718, never having got over her loss, and lies buried in Bucklebury church. Her ghost is said to haunt the vicarage, and is seen at least once a year.

There is no evidence to support a theory that Lord Bolingbroke had run off with another woman, and the reason for his departure was pursuit by government officers out to arrest him. He was the victim of his own political intrigue. A brilliant statesman, he drew up the Treaty of Utrecht in 1713, putting an end to the war with France. Queen Anne occupied the throne of England and did nothing to restrain Bolingbroke from pursuing the policies of the High Tory landed gentry. He put continuous pressure on religious dissenters to conform to the teachings of the established Church of England, and passed a law preventing anyone from standing for parliament unless they had an income from land of at least £300 a year. This made life very comfortable for the aristocracy and the fox-hunting squires, but Bolingbroke became exceedingly unpopular with everyone else; and the opprobrium was bound to rub off on his innocent wife, Frances.

In the dying days of Queen Anne, Bolingbroke forced new laws to exclude all but High Tories from any kind of power in parliament, the army or the church. On 1st August 1714 the queen was dead, and all the carefully contrived plans of Henry St John, Viscount Bolingbroke, lay in ruins, his supremacy removed overnight. As his friend Jonathan Swift said 'Fortune turned rotten at the very moment it grew ripe'. With the ascendency of the Whigs after Anne's death Swift returned to Dublin and lived the rest of his life in Ireland.

Queen Anne died without a successor, and the dour Prince George of Hanover came over from Germany to be crowned king. He was the great-grandson of James I. His grandmother had married Frederick, the Elector of the Rhineland Palatinate; and the somewhat bemused George, who spoke not one word of English, suddenly found himself king of England.

The new king had a deep distrust of the Tories, and the House of Hanover soon found itself hand in glove with their opponents, the Whig Party. The Tories remained in the political wilderness for the next 47 years. Bolingbroke was hounded out of the country, and lived abroad as adviser to the banished Stuarts, the 'Pretenders to the Throne'. He died an unhappy man in 1751.

Bucklebury also saw its fair share of other unsavoury habits, such as sheep stealing and body snatching. At one time, grisly thieves did a good trade by digging up freshly buried bodies and selling them for medical research to unscrupulous doctors. It was common practice for these body snatchers to frighten away hapless villagers by pretending to be ghosts.

The ploy was very effective, and superstitious locals gave churchyards a wide berth at night, for fear of being set upon by the restless spirits of the dead. One crafty bunch of thieves, having no bodies to dig up, made a good living from stealing sheep in the same spooky manner.

A farmer's son, annoyed at losses from his family's flock, and suspicious about the circumstances, decided to investigate. The rest of the village stayed with their flickering candles, behind the stout shutters of their kitchen windows. The young man crept out into the night, armed with a heavy club, and hid behind a tree. Soon he saw ghostly figures walking down the road towards him, carrying a coffin. He waited until the men drew abreast of the tree, then leapt out with a blood curdling shriek and lashed out with his club. The four men fled in terror. As their frightened footsteps faded into the distance, the young man bent down to examine the coffin.

It was very dark, and he was more than a little afraid. The wind made strange noises as it whistled through the trees, and there were rustlings in the undergrowth. A fox, perhaps, or a badger. He summoned up all his courage and put his hand on the lid of the coffin. He wrenched it open and found the carcass of a stolen sheep. With a great sigh of relief, and well pleased to have proved his theory right, he made his way back to the farm to get help.

The sheep stealing problem in Bucklebury ceased immediately, but the body snatching carried on. It was widespread, right up until this century, being the easiest way for hospitals and medical students to get cadavers for research. No doubt it was seen as a great humanitarian step forward when the practice ceased, and animals were substituted for medical experiments.

3

The Haunters of Newbury

N EWBURY Market Place is a lonely spot in the small hours of the morning. If buildings could speak, there would be a babble of stories of the past. But they can't and the only sound in the early hours is the wind as it moans eerily round the old masonry, picking up litter, only to dash it against a wall or shop front. The Market Place was the scene of countless humiliating public punishments. Murderers were hanged, thieves flogged and lesser felons put in the stocks or pillory.

In the 14th century, Sir Richard Abberbury founded Donnington Hospital and Priory. The priory is now the offices and salerooms of Dreweatt Neate, the auctioneers and valuers. The hospital survives, across the road, and is an almshouse, endowed to look after 13 poor men.

In 1538, one of the residents of the almshouses, Thomas Barrie, was accused of spreading seditious libel against the king, monastery-busting Henry VIII. The officers of the watch marched up from the town and arrested Barrie at dawn. He was taken in chains to the Market Place and put in the stocks. Barrie was an elderly man and was not in robust health – the forced march from Donnington nearly killed him.

The captain of the guard was a vicious brute, and was not content to see Barrie merely locked up with the crowd jeering at him. He ordered his men to pin Barrie's ears to the wooden framework of the stocks. The old man screamed with pain as the soldiers put the huge iron nails through his ears.

Barrie suffered in the stocks until sundown. Every time he

moved, the blood ran from his punctured ears and he cried with the pain. The brutish captain came back as the sun set over the cattle pens – now the site of the Kennet Centre – and told the old man he would be set free. Barrie begged for the nails to be taken out of his ears. The captain's reply was swift and merciless. Without a word, he drew his sword and sliced off both the old man's ears. Thomas Barrie died of shock. The old man's ghost is said to walk on dark nights, moaning with the pain of the barbaric treatment meted out to him.

One of Newbury's least known ghosts is the lady of the Pelican Theatre, founded by impresario Henry Thornton in 1802. The building was in Pelican Lane and is long gone. In the theatrical heyday of the last century, it was the venue for many productions, most of which were professionally staged by travelling theatre companies.

The story goes that the leading man of one particular production fell in love with his leading lady. He wooed her unsuccessfully; being in love with another man she spurned his advances. The actor plotted to get even, and one night as the final curtain fell and the players made to leave the stage for the dressing room, he turned and plunged a knife deep into the leading lady's bosom, crying 'If I can't have her, no man shall.' She collapsed, her dying words inaudible as she bled to death at the back of the stage. The actor fled. History does not record if he was brought to book for his heinous crime.

After the theatre closed, part of it was used as a house by a local family. The staircase to the bedrooms was on the other side of a wall from the stage where the actress was murdered. Before the advent of electricity, the family would take a candle to light their way up the stairs to bed. With alarming regularity, the candle would blow out on the top step – and relight itself as it was carried along the landing, away from the stage.

Later generations recorded that the electric bulb on the stairs would mysteriously blow as people made their way to bed. One visitor to the house replaced the light bulb three times before realising there was nothing physically wrong – the bulb proved to be perfectly all right when placed in other rooms.

One summer's evening, the lady of the house noticed a stain on the ceiling, as if water had been leaking in. A houseproud woman, she was curious as to how it could have got there. There had been no rain, and she did not know of any leaks in the roof. The stain grew, and appeared all the way down the wall, ending in a pool of liquid on the floor. She called her husband, and the couple looked curiously and uncomprehendingly at the phenomenon. The husband ran his hand down the wall and turned it to look at his palm. Both looked unbelievingly at the crimson stain running down his fingers. It was blood.

His wife bent down and put her finger in the pool on the floor, and looked closely at the drops that ran down her hand. There could be no doubt – she too was tainted with the phantom blood. The room was immediately below the stage where the actress had been murdered. The couple went into the kitchen and boiled up a large pan of water, and got some strong soap to remove the stain. But no amount of scrubbing would take it away, and the couple's hands were still stained crimson when they went to bed that evening.

After a sleepless night, morning finally came, bringing sunshine and the sound of bird song. They looked at their hands. There was nothing – all traces of the phantom stain had disappeared. They could think of no explanation for the phenomenon, other than a visitation from the spirit world.

The old theatre is no more, and nothing further was heard of the ghostly actress after the building was demolished. The site was subsequently built on, and is now offices. The spirit of the murdered woman seems to have been laid to rest – for the time being.

Dr Watson had his surgery in Northbrook Street, above what used to be Bateman's the opticians, across the alleyway from the Oxfam shop. He died over 100 years ago, and no one remembers much about him. Time passed and everyone forgot about the doctor, who had been a familiar sight in the town, with his tall black top hat and long black cloak. Nothing more was heard of him for 50 years – then he came back.

One dark, still night in wartime Britain, when the blackout meant there were no lights showing anywhere, a policeman was on duty at the Clock Tower. Nothing moved and there was not a sound. The policeman's boots scraped on the pavement as he turned to look down the Broadway towards Northbrook Street, and his heavy coat rustled with the movement. The noises crackled through the still night air, and the policeman's eyes opened wide as a silent figure drew close to him. Walking up the street was an old man, dressed in a top hat and a long dark cloak.

The bobby moved towards the shadowy figure to challenge him. As he reached out, it disappeared, leaving him clutching at thin air. Then he realised he had heard no footsteps, not a sound in the silence of the night.

A calm and patient man, not given to flights of fancy, he told his colleagues, and it transpired that the story of the shadowy figure was not new – it had been seen by others.

After the war ended, the old surgery became a family home, and the doctor appeared more and more. He was seen one night walking across a bedroom floor, but was only visible from his knees upwards. Later, the family learned that the floor had been raised since the doctor's time. His ghost had been walking across the original floor.

His favourite place to appear was on the staircase, where he was seen many times. The building later became a café, and many customers saw or felt the doctor's presence.

When the old surgery became the Bandarlog Café in the 1970s a woman once complained angrily to proprietor Mrs Jenny Ganf. She was walking up the staircase when a man in a cape and a top hat came rushing down and nearly knocked her over. Mrs Ganf went apprehensively to investigate. No human being had descended the stairs; it was the doctor.

He was seen to walk down those stairs on many occasions while the building was used as a café. Even the Ganfs' family dog felt his presence and used to whimper and scratch the floor. A very cynical lady cleaner who rubbished the idea of a ghost turned white with terror when she saw the doctor quite clearly, descending the staircase with his silver topped cane and black surgery bag.

Today the building has been entirely refurbished; the inside was gutted and completely rebuilt. The shop downstairs is now occupied by a company selling gifts and greetings cards. The upstairs is bright, brand new offices. The staircase where Doctor Watson used to prowl is gone. Only time will tell if he is gone too. Ghosts don't like having their surroundings altered, and seem to fade away if changes are made.

History records that in past centuries there was an old nonconformist chapel in Newbury, with a small graveyard surrounding it, just across the river from where the salerooms of Day, Shergold and Herbert used to be. The saleroom buildings are still standing, but the chapel has gone.

Local people would not go near it at night for fear of the ghosts which they said rose up from the graveyard. Tormented souls were often seen and heard, and sudden whirlwinds would pick up heavy objects and hurl them through the air. Reports of piercing shrieks and rattling chains, with skeletons wrapped in winding sheets were not uncommon.

It is not surprising that congregations found it easy to resist the call to prayers at this spooky-sounding place. The town had two similar chapels quite nearby, and the faithful soon showed their preference for worshipping in a place where they would not be frightened out of their wits by ghouls from the grave. Before long, the chapel was deserted.

But the church elders were far too canny to just leave it to rot. Newbury's prosperity was founded on enterprise and thrift – it would be sinful to waste what was, to all intents and purposes, a perfectly good building. So the chapel was turned into a sort of youth hostel, to accommodate young people travelling through the town who needed a place to stay for a few nights. What would these young visitors know of the chapel's ghoulish past, or even care if they did know?

At first, it was a great success, so much so that more space was needed. The church authorities decided to expand the building, and some of the old graves were built over to provide a kitchen. The new extension was to prove a nightmare for the young residents.

Pots and pans, neatly placed on the shelves overnight, would be strewn all over the floor next morning. Loud footsteps would be heard in the building at dead of night. Investigations revealed nothing. News of the strange happenings in the building spread like wildfire, and the youth of Britain stayed away in droves. Once again the building was empty.

After the Second World War, it was purchased by Berkshire County Council. By this time, stories of the chapel's past had been largely forgotten, probably because the local population had far more pressing things to worry about, like the bombs which demolished St John's Church and the council school.

The county council ordered the building to be demolished. On the site, they would build a prestigious new youth centre – provided the budget would stretch to it. A local firm of architects was commissioned to draw up plans, and tenders for building work were put out. The architect went to the site, and came away with dark premonitions.

His name was Clyde Grube, and he was an American. He arrived in Newbury in 1944 as a US paratrooper of the 101st Airborne Division, and married a local girl. Instead of whisking her off to USA, the couple settled down in Newbury.

'The first problem we had with this site was that it had a lot of old burial vaults,' he said. 'None of them were marked, and some of them were very large. We had a bulldozer clearing the site and it hit one of these underground chambers. It just disappeared straight into it. The driver got a shock, but he wasn't hurt. We had a heck of a job getting the machine back out of the hole.'

That was just for starters. The council was pressing for work to get under way as speedily as possible, and no extra money was available for unforeseen problems – the budget was very tight. More holes appeared, sometimes empty, sometimes containing skeletons and corpses in advanced states of decomposition. All had to be carefully removed and reinterred. Work got further and further behind.

Even when the groundwork was complete and the structure started to go up, strange things would happen. Bricks, blocks and timber would move around the site as if by magic. One day, a lorry load of steel ties, used for reinforcing concrete, was delivered. A crane was brought in to unload them, and they were left carefully placed in a neat pile, ready for use. The workmen went home.

Mr Grube remembers coming onto the site first thing next morning. 'I could not believe what I saw,' he said. 'The whole pile had moved. It was as if a giant hand had come down, gently picked up several tons of steel and moved it a few feet. The pile was perfectly tidy – but it was in a different place.'

By now, a number of workmen had been spooked out by the strange happenings on the site and had handed in their notice. Mr Grube was there when one of them was frightened off by a paranormal visit.

The man was working alone on a part of the site when he felt someone tap him on the shoulder. He turned to see who had disturbed him, but there was no one there. He thought nothing of it and carried on working. A little later, he felt it again, this time more insistent. Again there was no one there. He carried on working. The next time the tap came, it was much harder, a quite severe blow.

By now, the workman was angry, and determined to get even with his tormentor. The only other person he could see was a bricklayer working at the other end of the site, over 50 yards away. The furious workman yelled at him, accusing him of a nasty practical joke. The startled bricklayer, totally innocent, denied all knowledge and shrugged his shoulders. The workman was not convinced, and started towards him,

24

uttering threats of retaliation. Mr Grube, foreseeing trouble, ran out to prevent the bricklayer from being attacked.

'I had seen the whole thing, and there was no way that anyone had gone near the man,' said Mr Grube. 'He was an Irishman, new on the site, and I explained to him some of the problems we had encountered. He went as white as a sheet and instantly handed in his notice to the foreman. He collected his stuff from his landlady and caught the next train back to Ireland.'

The building was finally completed, and became the Waterside Youth and Community Centre. Its new incarnation seems to have laid the ghosts of the past, and it is a popular venue for young people engaged in all sorts of activities. Despite being there for a number of years the manager of the centre, Mr Gunther Schwarz, knew nothing of the building's past, and reports no ghostly activity in the building whatsoever – but he would like to know what makes all the table tennis balls vanish...

4

Echoes of the
Civil War

THE ghosts of men killed in battle are said to march again in troubled times, and their spirits cannot rest until their death is avenged. Whole armies are buried under the soil of Berkshire. But the ghosts of men-at-arms are probably the least troublesome of earthbound spirits. There are many reports of their hauntings, but these lost souls are always well-disciplined and cause few problems for those who come after them – apart from being a rather nasty shock.

Battles in Berkshire date back to prehistoric times. The county has been consistently fought over by successions of different tribes, conquered by the Roman Empire, and fought over during the Dark Ages, when it was successively invaded by Celts, Saxons, Angles, and Jutes from northern Europe.

Then came the Danes. They marched west as far as Reading, where they set up a garrison. King Alfred – the one who burnt the cakes – was the English leader, and he routed the invaders in a series of victories, notably at Englefield, Ashdown, and on the Berkshire Downs near Goring in AD 871. Alfred chased the Danes back as far as Tilehurst, where they rallied and fought back. A fierce battle ensued, with bloody carnage on both sides. One of the roads in nearby Theale is still called Dead Man's Lane, a not uncommon road name in the county.

The Danes sallied forth again to fight Alfred at the Battle of Ashdown, where he defeated them after a long and hard fight. The Danes retreated to Basingstoke, a place in which Alfred was not interested. The kingdom of Wessex was safe, and gradually absorbed the remaining Danish invaders, who settled down to farm the lands, much the same as the Saxons had done before them. Viking raids continued on the coast and up rivers such as the Thames and Kennet, and people tended to build their homes slightly away from the roads and waterways. It is a fairly common feature for main roads between towns to be almost devoid of population; but roadside signposts bear witness to small hamlets, hidden out of sight, a mile or so away from the main thoroughfare.

William the Conqueror arrived in 1066, and the Saxons found themselves labouring under the Norman yoke. Again, time allowed the Normans to integrate into the existing society, and a peace of sorts reigned for hundreds of years.

When Charles I came to the throne in 1625, he believed in the divine right of kings, that he was appointed by God, and that no man could depose him, no matter how badly he behaved. The English Civil War was to prove him wrong. After years of brother fighting against brother, Charles was defeated and beheaded in Whitehall.

There were famous battles in West Berkshire in 1643 and 1644, some of the most fearsome of the whole war, and stories abound of earthbound spirits from this era – spirits which have never come to terms with their horrific and untimely end. There is no shortage of Roundhead and Cavalier ghosts haunting the countryside.

The Hesketh sisters came from Lancashire to settle in Newbury. The elder of the two, who lived at Biggs Cottage, Enborne, was the cook at Park House School. She often saw the ghost of the Earl of Essex, the Roundhead general at the First Battle of Newbury, walking slowly through the cottage. She described him as a serious looking man who wore a broad brimmed hat with a flat top.

Her sister never saw a thing, and derided the whole idea. Years later, after the elder sister died, the younger one was to eat her words as the Earl appeared to her – exactly as her sister had described. He had stayed at the old cottage before the battle, in which 6,000 men were cut to death in the service of their opposing causes.

27

The sentry outside the general's headquarters has been seen, and traditionally appears on the anniversary of the battle. A woman riding a horse past the cottage on the eve of the anniversary some years ago had to detour round the cottage – the frightened animal would not go past it, although the woman rider saw nothing.

The battle proved horrendous, and the bodies of the slain were piled on top of each other at nearby Cope Hall. The mansion has since been demolished, but even now the site has an eerie and ghostly feeling. In the past, some people have claimed to witness scenes from the battle at its fiercest, relating accounts of blood-curdling horror.

The late Lt Col John Ramsey-Fairfax recalled before his death, 'A school friend of mine had an aunt who was stone deaf. One Sunday, after lunch, she went upstairs to rest. At about three o'clock she came rushing downstairs, calling out that there must be an accident or something dreadful happening outside. Couldn't they hear the shouting, the horses neighing – even the sound of cannon fire?

'They had quite a job calming her down; no one else had heard a thing. But they discovered later that the date was the anniversary of the battle. The aunt remained stone deaf.'

Many people lost loved ones on both sides during the battles of Newbury. Philip Weston was a Royalist and lived at Bussock House, long since demolished, near Winterbourne. His daughter was in love with a Roundhead officer. During the second battle, her father arranged a signal to let his daughter know how the fight had gone. If her father was killed, she would hear a single trumpet blast. Two blasts meant her lover was dead. Three meant both had died.

The girl waited with apprehension, wringing her hands with grief as she waited for the signal as the sounds of the battle grew gradually quieter. Three shrill blasts rent the deathly silence that followed the bloody battle. The distraught girl, robbed of the two men who meant most to her, threw herself down a well. Her ghost is said to walk the neighbourhood on moonless nights.

The quiet suburban street of Falkland Garth in Wash

Common stands next to the house where one of the Royalist commanders, Lord Falkland, was hurriedly brought when he was fatally wounded in the battle of 20th September 1643.

Lucius Cary, Viscount Falkland, was Secretary of State, and a loyal patriot. He seemed to have a premonition of his impending death, for he received Holy Communion on the morning of the battle, saying 'I am weary of the times, and foresee much misery to my country; but I believe I shall be out of it ere night.' The Civil War memorial at Wash Common commemorates him and his comrades in arms, 'The blameless and the brave'.

Lord Falkland has been seen countless times walking through the old manor house. The Henshaw family lived there for many years and, as is a common thread in stories of the paranormal, the family dog sensed his lordship's presence, and refused to sleep in the kitchen where Lord Falkland died.

The cook, described as a 'cheerful extrovert', saw his lordship as she laboured over her pots and pans. She described him as 'a short man, dressed in black'. She identified the ghost as Lord Falkland from a contemporary portrait.

Another Royalist victim was the Earl of Carnarvon, the cavalry commander. He had that morning measured a gateway with his sword, to see if it was wide enough to march through all the prisoners which the Earl was quite convinced would be taken by the king's men before nightfall. Although the horsemen of Carnarvon and Prince Rupert inflicted severe damage on Parliament's troops, Carnarvon was to fall in a reckless cavalry charge, and his corpse was carried through the same gateway that evening.

Prince Rupert of the Rhine was the stuff of romantic legend. A German prince born in Prague, he was the grandson of James I, and came to England at the age of 22 to help his uncle, King Charles. His exploits during the Civil War were legion, and history records him as a flamboyant and brilliant cavalry commander. After the war, he employed his talents as a sea captain, and went to live in Canada to become governor of the Hudson's Bay Company.

After the indecisive First Battle of Newbury, the Parliamentary troops, short of stores and ammunition, retired towards their stronghold in London. Rupert and his Cavaliers harried them as far as Theale, where a fierce skirmish took place. Once again the victims of battle were buried in Dead Man's Lane, a narrow track with no buildings on either side.

Phantom battle re-enactments are not uncommon stories in the weird and wonderful world of the paranormal. One such story tells of a Royalist cavalry patrol attacked at night on their way to Donnington Castle, which was held for the king, by a superior force of Parliamentary troops. Three Cavalier officers were killed in bloody hand to hand combat.

The incident bears a close resemblance to the phantom battle of Marston Moor, a phenomenon which many people claim to have seen. Newbury's version is said to take place on the old showground at Love Lane.

While the town was occupied by the Parliamentary troops in 1643, they chased and killed a woman who was thought to be a witch. A contingent of Roundheads based in the town centre saw a woman apparently walking on the water of the river Kennet. They chased her, intending to seize her as a witch, but she outpaced them. They started shooting. The soldiers' account of the incident says she laughed derisively at them and caught their bullets in her hands – then chewed them up as if they were tasty morsels.

Finally, one soldier, braver than the rest, got near enough to cut a slash across her forehead with his sword. This was believed to be a sure way of dealing with sorcery, and the soldier then shot her at point blank range under her ear, rumoured to be an effective way of killing a witch. Sure enough, 'She sunk strait down and died', as the military record states. 'Her soul we ought not to judge of, though the evils of her wicked life and death can escape no censure.'

The witch's body was dragged out of the river next to the small chapel where, in years to come, the congregation was so disturbed by paranormal activity that the building was abandoned.

5

The Spectral Soldier

IT was the custom of Captain Edward Purvis to sit at his window in Reading and watch the world go by. So much so that his persona was imprinted onto his surroundings, and the captain's ghost was seen at his window in Watlington Street long after his death, wearing his red military tunic, his hair in a pigtail, and smoking a long clay pipe.

Captain Purvis was a veteran of the Spanish Peninsular War, when British soldiers under the Duke of Wellington drove the French forces out of Spain to liberate it from the yoke of Emperor Napoleon.

Purvis had been an officer at the Battle of Corunna, on the north-west coast of Spain, and had a close call when a Frenchman put a bullet through his hat. Another Reading soldier, Joshua Hawkins, whose family lived near St Giles Church in Southampton Street – known in those days as Horn Street – told of how the British General, Sir John Moore, was killed at the Battle of Corunna.

Hawkins was a soldier in the 7th Hussars, which was made up almost entirely of Reading men. They spent Christmas Day in 1808 on a hillside watching the French army under Marshal Soult advancing towards the British positions. Hawkins and his comrades were miserable because they could not get anything to eat, and Christmas Day brought them no festivities whatsoever.

At dusk, the hungry men resolved to ride down into a small town to sample the hospitality of their Spanish hosts, whose king had promised undying support for his allies.

The townspeople had other ideas, and told the soldiers there was nothing for them. The disgruntled Hussars got off their horses and went into the inn with swords drawn. There they found bread and wine and sat down to eat. By this time a mob had gathered outside, and the Hussars had to finish their meal in the saddle to escape the angry Spaniards, who were pelting them with stones.

Captain Purvis survived the Peninsular War and returned to his home town to retire, although he joined the ranks of Berkshire's part time militia, and soon became its adjutant. He married and settled down at Watlington House.

Samuel Watlington, a local clothmaker, had the house built towards the end of the 17th century, beside the track which led to the south side of what had been Reading Abbey. The house was later extended, and parts of it and the surrounding wall were built with flints taken from the abbey ruins. After the Purvis family moved away, the house became a girls' school, and the headmistress was a Mrs Stevens. In 1877, Kendrick School for girls was established there by Reading Corporation, using endowments left by cloth merchant John Kendrick, who died in 1624, and Mary Kendrick, who died in 1713 at the age of 21.

Captain Purvis went off to Ireland with the militia and returned home to Reading with them in 1815. This meant he was not present at the Battle of Waterloo, in which many townsmen fought, including Joshua Hawkins' brother, Sergeant Caleb Hawkins of the 14th Light Dragoons. He sent an account of the battle to his sister, and it was read aloud to the people on the steps of the post office in London Street. For many years after, Waterloo was a favourite name for new roads and buildings, and Reading still has a Waterloo Road, off Elgar Road, and Wellington Avenue, off Shinfield Road.

But Purvis was there when Napoleon's state coach, pulled by four horses, was brought to Reading, accompanied by his coachman and valet, both of whom had served Napoleon at Waterloo, with the valet losing an arm in the battle. Crowds flocked to see the emperor's gilded carriage, and it was put on show in the Forbury for several days.

Purvis was remembered as a gallant officer and a genial

friend. He became the town's senior magistrate and was a churchwarden at St John's Church in Watlington Street, which is now Reading's Polish Catholic Church. The town has a large and well respected Polish contingent, many of whom came here to fight with the British forces in the Second World War, having escaped from the domination of their country by the Nazis in 1939, and subsequently stayed here to escape the domination of the Russians in 1945.

After Napoleon's defeat by Wellington and Blucher at Waterloo in 1815, he was exiled to the remote island of St Helena in the South Atlantic, where he was guarded night and day. Napoleon had escaped once before from captivity, and his English jailers were taking no chances. He died there in 1821.

A mood of peace had settled over England, and the army found many of its regiments reduced or disbanded. The Berkshire Militia suffered such a fate, and all that was left of it was its drum and fife band, which used to practise on the meadow next to Captain Purvis' house in Watlington Street. The captain, by now an elderly gentleman, would without fail sit at his window, smoking his pipe, to watch them being put through their paces by Sergeant-Major Preston.

The band soon became famous for its marching displays, and contained a number of very fine musicians. On Sunday mornings, they would march from the Forbury to St Lawrence's Church, playing *Hark, the Bonnie Christ Church Bells*, much to the delight of the crowd which always gathered to watch them.

The meadow where the band used to practise has now been built on, but the ghost of Captain Purvis still sees them in his memory, as he sits at the window with his pipe.

6

The Spirit of Winding Wood

ALL Souls Night, according to the old pagan myths, is when the dead rise up from their graves to walk the earth. A young school teacher met a ghost on All Souls Night during the last war. First hand accounts like this are very rare; here is her amazing story.

Mrs Rosemary Stevens is the daughter of Mr Oswald Harman Smith, who was a well known accountant in Newbury. When war broke out in 1939 the family was living near London airport, but returned to Berkshire in 1940 to escape the heavy bombing. They went to live at Winding Wood farmhouse, a lonely spot to the north of the A4 near Kintbury.

'It was an exciting time at my mother's home at Winding Wood, if a little frightening,' said Mrs Stevens. 'The Americans were always on manoeuvres, and planes would fly overhead with men in parachutes tumbling out. Tanks would rumble along the lanes, and there would be soldiers in foxholes in the woods. There was a huge searchlight across the field. It would send its light high in the sky, looking for aeroplanes. They were getting ready for the Normandy landings.

'One beautiful summer's day in 1942, when I was six years old, a Wellington bomber zoomed low overhead. It was obviously in trouble, and got lower and lower. It went out of sight over the woods, and we heard an almighty crash. My father went immediately to call for help. The plane had broken in two when it hit the ground in Three Gates Wood.

'We found out afterwards it was on a training flight, with a Canadian crew. When he realised the plane was in trouble, the pilot had ordered the crew up to the cockpit. The rear gunner didn't make it in time and he was killed on impact. The air force came and took him away, and a little while later they came back to remove the wreck of the plane.'

There is no report of the crash in the wartime editions of the local paper, the *Newbury Weekly News*. Censorship was very strictly imposed during the war, and newspapers were not allowed to report events of this nature because the government believed it was bad for morale and could give sensitive information to the enemy. Even when Newbury was bombed by a German plane, news reports said the bombs fell 'somewhere in the south of England'.

Mrs Stevens told how she spent her childhood at Winding Wood, and went to work at nearby Denford Park. 'Many years later, I was working at Denford Park as a trainee teacher,' she said. 'I must have been about 20 years old. This was before it became Norland, and in those days it was a very exclusive school. One evening at the beginning of November, I was walking home to Winding Wood. It was getting dark, the last bit of twilight. I was walking down the road at Cox's Corner and had almost reached the spot where plane came down at Three Gates Wood. When I was a few yards from the spot, something made me look up into the elm trees. There was an eerie sort of misty light up at the top – about 30 feet high. I looked at the light. At first, I thought it might be an owl. After a few minutes I saw it develop into the shape of a man, a big man – and I could see straight through him.

'I didn't know what to do. Should I run – or hide? It was a long way home and I walked there very smartly. I was more than a little concerned at what I had just seen. My mother laughed at me. She was a very down to earth country woman.

'I went to work at the school next day, and the Reverend Mother came and spoke to me. She could see I was troubled, but I was nervous about telling her what I had seen. But I told her what had happened – it was a bit embarrassing, but she listened quietly and patiently.

"Do you know what night it was last night?" asked the kindly nun, very gently.

"No, Reverend Mother," I replied, bemused. "It was All Souls Night," said Reverend Mother. Then I realised what I had seen,' said Mrs Stevens. 'It was the Canadian airman at Cox's Corner. I never saw him again. I told my uncle, Toby Sutton, but none of the family ever sighted the airman again.'

Her story is not widely known, and even some local people are unaware of it. Mrs Stevens said her experience had not made her frightened of the supernatural, and she dealt with the whole episode in a very matter of fact way, just as one would expect of a traditional schoolmarm.

She did, however, suggest that psychic phenomena may be far more common than people realise.

'It's quite possible there are lots of ghosts walking about, quite visibly, but people just don't realise they are ghosts and not real people.'

She cited the case of the guide at Littlecote House who was standing at the door, collecting visitors' tickets as they went in. She smiled at the last woman in the queue as she hurried towards the door, and asked for her ticket. The stylishly dressed woman completely ignored her, and carried on walking – straight through the wall.

Although Mrs Stevens is unusual in having the gift of what might be called 'second sight', she is by no means unique. Another woman of my acquaintance, whom I came to regard with considerable respect, is Mrs Jeanne Grube, who lived in Newbury for many years. I was in the habit of meeting and talking periodically on the telephone with her and her husband. After not speaking to them for several weeks, I rang Mrs Grube to ask for her help with trying to understand something about psychic phenomena. She answered the telephone and knew who was calling before I had chance to speak a word. 'I knew it was you, I was expecting you,' she said.

7

The Kintbury Witch

Bells have long been regarded as having special powers. Churches rang them, not only to summon the congregation, but to keep away evil spirits. The bell at Kintbury church rang the chimes every hour, on the hour – an unwelcome din to insomniacs in the middle of a long winter's night, until the bell tower was struck by lightning and the bell was silenced. Local people blamed the village witch.

No one knew the witch's name. Legend tells that she lived in a tiny hovel at a place called Three Cornered Hat, near Tinker's Corner, and earned a living as a chimney sweep with her long and magical broom. She dressed in sackcloth and her face was lined with soot. The superstitious village people were convinced she could do magic, and she was reputed to cast spells on anyone who incurred her displeasure. She turned detective to identify a thief who stole some silver spoons, and forced him to return them. A carter who refused to give her a lift was amazed when his horses became rooted to the spot. He agreed to take her if she would remove the spell, and the horses promptly moved off.

Although the villagers were proud of their great bell, its loudness was not its most endearing feature. Windows rattled and crockery jumped when the clock struck the hour. Every time babies cried or milk went sour, the bell would be blamed.

One summer's evening, as the last rays of the setting sun were chased away by fast moving clouds, distant thunder rumbled in the treetops, and the rain began to fall. As darkness fell, a fierce thunderstorm enveloped the village, and a huge bolt of lightning hit the church tower, splitting it in half. The great bell was ripped from its beam; it tore away from its mountings and crashed to the ground, banging and clanging as it fell. Bouncing heavily it rolled downhill towards the river, ending up in the water with an almighty splash, sinking slowly in the mud until only the tip of its top could be seen.

The people were terrified. They thought the witch had done this wicked deed, perhaps out of spite. Some said they had seen her riding her broomstick at the height of the storm, cackling insanely, as the bell rolled towards the river. Everyone agreed the bell would have to be recovered.

The village elders, convinced that witchcraft had been invoked, decided to seek the advice of a magician. Some distance away lived a hermit who was reputed to have mystical powers, and a delegation was sent to ask him what to do.

The delegation spent a long time with the hermit, who stroked his beard and shook his head. He looked at his magical books and read the stars, and still shook his head. The delegation upped the fee. 'Perhaps,' said the hermit. When the fee rose high enough, he suddenly found a solution.

The delegation returned to the village with a plan of action. A brand new steel chain was to be hitched to the bell, which was to be pulled out of the river by a team of 12 snow white heifers, each one to be led by a maiden dressed in white. The ceremony was to commence at midnight, and most important of all, it had to be conducted in complete silence. If anyone uttered so much as a grunt, the spell would be broken and the bell would sink below the waters for ever.

The hermit was probably a legendary wise man who lived at Crookham Common. His name was Coudrey, and he had exceptional powers. The story goes that a thief once came into Coudrey's garden to steal cabbages. While he was in the act of pulling them up, he was enveloped in a sudden and unexplained flood of water. The man was drowned, and Coudrey disposed of his body next morning, by which time the flood had subsided. Another foolish thief tried to take some blocks of wood which Coudrey had stored behind his house. Suddenly he found himself transported inside the building, face to face with the wizard. A carter who had lost a pony went to Coudrey to ask his help in finding it. The wise man told him there would be a great storm, and he had better hurry home. He would find the pony; but would regret it. The carter looked at the cloudless blue sky, shrugged his shoulders, and started for home. Within minutes, a storm blew up. The rain came down in bucketfuls, and with it, the pony. It fell out of the sky onto the carter's head, killing him instantly.

When Coudrey had reached a great age and was dying, he said 'Much has been done by scholarship. But I have had dealings with the devil.'

The moon shone brightly as the Kintbury villagers made their silent way to the river bank, a spot still known as 'The Bell Hole', near Barton Court. The new chain was shackled to the top of the bell and the heifers began to heave. The chain went taut and the bell eased slowly out of the mud. Just as the maidens silently urged their beasts for one final pull, a voice rang out. It was the witch.

She stood by the river, dressed in her sackcloth and heavy boots. Her body was bent with age and her sunken eyes looked out over a long bent nose which almost touched her toothless chin.

'Here again comes the Kintbury Bell, in spite of all the devils in hell!' she cackled.

The chain snapped and the bell sank into the depths of the river. The spell was broken. The villagers ran for their lives and locked their doors behind them, lest the evil should follow them home.

As she stood on the river bank, it slowly dawned upon the witch that her outburst would make her even more unpopular than she was already. The people had run off in abject fear, but in the morning, they would be back, their resolve stiffened by daylight and self-righteous anger. She went back to her hovel to collect her few meagre possessions and was never seen again. The bell suffered the same fate, and is believed to be hidden still beneath the murky waters of the Kennet. Legend has it that whenever the bells peal in the rebuilt church tower, the great bell booms out a ghostly echo from its watery grave.

Great excitement gripped the village some years ago, when a group of young men announced they had found the bell and were going to recover it. Ropes and winches were rigged up by the riverside as they heaved with all their might to bring the bell to the surface. This was no ceremony with snow white heifers, it was a show of brute force. Sinews rippled as a large object bubbled to the surface – but it was not the bell. It was an old 40-gallon metal drum, full of water. A disappointed crowd wandered off, resigned to the notion that the great bell would never be seen again.

Superstition suggests that the witch, who disappeared on the night she broke the spell, crawled into the water and under the bell to escape the people's wrath. Legend has it that she is still there, hanging onto the clapper, waiting to bewitch anyone who tries to pull the bell out of the water...

But there was a happy ending for St Mary's Church at Kintbury. In 1994, a group of villagers got together to refurbish the bells and add another, in memory of Sir Gordon Richards, the famous jockey. Lots of money was needed for the project, and vigorous fund-raising by Mrs Billee Chapman Pincher, who lives next door to the church and is married to the famous spy writer, soon brought in the five figure sum necessary. In the spring of 1995, Mrs Chapman Pincher was joined by Her Majesty Queen Elizabeth II for a dedication ceremony for the new bell.

8

The Phantom Highwaymen

During the hours of daylight it seems unlikely that a busy motorway junction could be haunted. But at night, under the eerie light of the big orange lamps, the silence is oppressive, and the approach of a solitary vehicle is more menacing than reassuring. But, worse still, imagine yourself there in total darkness.

Before the motorway came, Maidenhead Thicket was a very spooky place indeed. The tarmac ribbon of the A4 is bounded on both sides by thickly growing trees and bushes. Night-time traffic was sparse, and to be alone and on foot was a frightening experience.

Because of the excellent cover provided by the natural foliage, the thicket was the favourite stamping ground for highwaymen for miles around, and the ghosts of two of them are reputed to haunt the road, still in search of the rich pickings they once enjoyed; although these spectral figures must be much puzzled by the fast cars and articulated juggernauts which have replaced the plodding stagecoaches they were so fond of robbing.

The most famous of the thicket's highwaymen was Claude Duval, a Frenchman born in the town of Domfront, Normandy, in 1643. He arrived in England to escape the French authorities in 1660 with a price on his head and was to enjoy a ten year career of robbery – but not violence. Duval became known as the most courteous highwayman in England, and his legend was revered in every tavern.

The exploit which really made his name happened at Maidenhead Thicket in about 1665, when he stopped a coach belonging to a rich man who was carrying a purse of golden sovereigns. The incident was made famous when a shrewd publisher printed the story a transcript of which has survived to this day. This is how the story was told.

'Duval, with his squadron, overtook a coach which they had set overnight, having intelligence of a booty of £400 in it. In the coach was a knight, his lady and one serving maid, who, perceiving five horsemen making up to them, presently imagined that they were beset; and they were confirmed in this apprehension by seeing them whisper to one another, and ride backwards and forwards. The lady, to show she was not afraid, took a small flute from her pocket and proceeded to play it. Duval took the hint and played also, most excellently well, on a small flute of his own.

'He rode up to the side of the coach and said to the knight, "Sir, your lady plays excellently, and I doubt not but that she dances as well. Will you please to walk out of the coach and let me have the honour to dance one dance with her?"

"Sir," said the knight, "I dare not deny anything to one of your quality and good manners. You seem a gentleman, and your request is very reasonable."

'The door of the coach opened, and out stepped the knight. Duval sprang lightly from his horse and handed the lady out of the coach. They danced, and here it was that Duval performed marvels; the best masters in London, except those that are French, not being able to show such footing as he did in his great French riding boots. The dancing being over (with no violins, Duval sang the music himself), he waits on the lady to her coach. As the knight was getting back in, Duval said to him "Sir, you have forgotten to pay for the music."

"No, I have not," replied the knight, and, putting his hand under the seat of the coach, pulled out a bag containing £100, which Duval took with very good grace, and courteously answered "Sir, you are liberal, and shall have no cause to repent your being so. This liberality of yours shall excuse you from the other £300 which you have in your possession."'

Doffing his three cornered hat, Duval gave the knight a password to use if he was stopped by other highwaymen further up the road. Despite his good manners, Duval was not a man to be crossed. He was an expert swordsman and shot, and was unbeaten at duelling.

Highwaymen often got news of who was travelling on the road from Bath to London from the inns where the travellers stayed overnight. Gang members would stay at the same places, not only observing the travellers' movements, but also bribing the servants for information, particularly of how much money was being carried.

One of Duval's favourite haunts was the Black Boy Inn at Slough, which used to be opposite where the public library now stands. The origins of its name are grisly, to say the least. The innkeeper at the time had the perfectly preserved body of a Negro boy in a glass case in the hallway. Reputedly, he bought it from Sir Robert Vyner, whose wife made him get rid of it from their home at Ickenham in Middlesex. The sight of it so shocked the famous diarist Samuel Pepys that he made a note of it in his diary on 7th September 1665, 'He showed me a black boy that he had, that had died of consumption; and being dead, he caused him to be dried in an oven, and is there entire in a box.' The Black Boy was demolished in 1910, and the bricks were used for making pathways in the garden of a Mr Bentley, who had his home at Upton.

The inn was well placed for Duval because it was halfway between Hounslow Heath, which was ideal for robbing travellers leaving London on the journey to Bath, and Maidenhead Thicket, which was ideal for robbing them on the way back again. For many years, clergymen in the Maidenhead area had to be given extra protection against highwaymen, and many of them got so fed up with being robbed they either refused to travel on the Bath Road, or else demanded extra payment.

Hounslow Heath had 13 gibbets along the roadside, in order to discourage robbers, and there were always bodies hanging from them. George III complained that the sight –

and smell – of them upset him on his frequent journeys to Windsor Castle, and they were removed in 1800.

Duval operated his territory with Jack Rann and John Cottington. The latter achieved great fame in his own right when he robbed an army pay coach. He got away with £40,000, an enormous amount of money in those days.

Duval was eventually caught, and on 21st January 1670 was hanged on the gallows at Tyburn. He was 27 years old, and hugely famous. Thousands turned out to see their hero's inglorious end, and after he was hanged, his body lay in state for several days in the Tangier Tavern in St Giles, and people flocked to see it. Understandably outraged, the authorities quickly arranged for the body to be buried. Duval's last resting place is in the centre of the aisle in Covent Garden church, under a stone inscribed 'Here lies Duval. Reader, if male thou art, look to thy purse; if female, to thy heart.'

Two other infamous highwaymen followed in Duval's hoof prints on the Bath Road. Dick Turpin was famous for his speed, and seemed to be everywhere at once. He had a secret room in the Old Lambe Inn at Theale, but is best known for his epic ride from London to York. The other robber who haunts Maidenhead Thicket is reputed to be Captain Hawkes, 'The Flying Highwayman', who was an ingenious villain and a master of disguise. His most famous exploit took place at the Plough Inn at Salt Hill, on the Bath Road to the west of Slough.

A merchant swaggered in, loudly and rudely demanding service. He placed two horse-pistols on the bar and boasted he would never fall victim to robbers on the road. The only other occupant in the room was a man dressed in the sober suit and broad hat of a Quaker, quietly eating his bread and cheese. The man carried on bragging that he would see all highwaymen hang – or shoot them himself with his own pistols. He walked up and down the room, boasting at the top of his voice, and then sat down in a far corner with his back to the Quaker and started to count his money.

The Quaker rose silently to pay his bill and depart. He

walked up to the bar and placed coins on it, next to the braggart's pistols. Then he went.

The boisterous traveller followed soon afterwards in his carriage. After about a mile, the carriage was stopped. A black-masked face appeared at the window, accompanied by a pistol, and a voice uttered 'Your money or your life!'

The traveller already had his horse-pistols in his hands, and raised them to the robber's head. He fired them both at once, but to his disgust, instead of a loud explosion, all he got was two clicks as flint hit metal. The masked man roared with laughter.

'No good, my friend,' he said. 'The powder was blown out of thy pans, almost under thy nose. If thou dost not want a bullet through thy head, hand over the purse in thy hat, the banknotes in thy fob, the gold snuffbox and the diamond ring up thy sleeve.'

The highwayman's pistol was at the traveller's head, the trigger at full cock. He had no choice, and handed over all the valuables demanded by the masked robber, who cheekily handed him back a single coin, saying 'There is enough to pay your turnpike. In future, don't brag so much.'

He turned his horse's head and was gone, the light slowly dawning on the dim-witted boaster that the meek-mannered Quaker at the inn was none other than Captain Hawkes.

Hawkes was hoist by his own petard later that day. He rode over 20 miles to the Rising Sun Inn at Woolhampton, where he dismounted and strode wearily into the bar. Two ploughmen were there, both wearing workers' smocks, and squabbling about whose turn it was to buy beer. As Captain Hawkes sipped his gin and water, the two ploughmen came to blows, and one of them drew a knife.

The highwayman intervened, and seized the man's arm in his powerful grasp. To his amazement, the man jumped free, and the other had the captain's wrists in handcuffs. The rustic smocks fell away to reveal the red tunics of the Bow Street Runners. The infamous Captain Hawkes was caught.

So if you have the misfortune to meet a ghostly highwayman at Maidenhead Thicket, and he is polite and charming, you may be sure it is Claude Duval. Ladies have nothing to fear, as long as they can dance a little, and gentlemen will merely be relieved of their money. But beware the ghostly figure of Captain Hawkes, master of disguise. Who knows what he may appear as next. Could he have been that mild-mannered man you met in the pub just down the road? He was talking about golf, and said he was going shooting...

9

A Child's Handprint

THE Royal Stag pub at Datchet has one of the most eerie phenomena in the county. From time to time, and totally without warning, a spectral handprint becomes visible on one of the windows.

According to legend, the print is made by the ghost of a young boy, vainly trying to attract the attention of the people in the warm and comfortable hostelry. The story goes that the lad was taken to the pub by his father, a village labourer in Victorian times.

It was deep midwinter, and snow lay thick on the ground. The landlord would not let the boy inside, and his father told him to wait while he drank his ale. The boy wandered into the graveyard immediately next door and tried to amuse himself. It was bitterly cold, and the mischievous attraction of throwing snowballs at gravestones soon palled. He ran around in the snow to keep warm, but quickly became tired in the intense cold, and went to the light of the alehouse window to look for his father.

The man seemed to have completely forgotten about his young son, and stayed inside, drinking. By now the boy was pitifully cold, and tapped on the window to try and attract someone's attention. His last desperate act was to push the window pane with his hand. The print froze on the glass. Exhausted, he fell asleep in the snow in the graveyard. By the time he was found he had frozen to death.

And so the boy's ghostly handprint appears periodically on the window. In 1979 a national newspaper told the story, accompanied by a photograph of the handprint. The newspaper got a local glazier to take out the pane of glass so it could be examined. The glazier replaced the window with a new one. The old glass was subjected to all sorts of scientific tests, but nothing was found. It was just an old window pane, and eventually the technicians had to admit there was nothing strange whatsoever about it.

But meanwhile, the handprint had appeared again – on the brand new pane of glass. It was a clear imprint of a left palm, fingers and thumb, quite small, almost certainly that of a young child.

Whatever was manifesting itself at the Royal Stag was obviously not happy with the reaction it was causing. One night a copy of the newspaper photograph was left on the bar, where locals had been examining and discussing it. Next morning the landlord came down to find broken glass everywhere. Bottles and glasses had been smashed all over the bar and on the floor – and no one had heard a thing. Tales of beer glasses moving about became common. Ghostly footsteps were heard frequently when there was no one there to make them, and strange noises were heard in the cellar.

Like so many other ghostly happenings, events at the Royal Stag are totally unpredictable and cannot usually be induced. Who knows when the mysterious handprint will appear again on the window? But you can be sure that when it happens, the TV cameras will be there as quickly as the newsmen can carry them. Ghosts make good stories, and even better television.

10

Herne the Hunter of Windsor Forest

THE Anglo Saxon Chronicle records in 1127 'Let no one be surprised at what we are about to relate, for it was common gossip up and down the countryside that after February 6, many people both saw and heard a whole pack of huntsmen in full cry. They straddled black horses and black bucks, while their hounds were pitch black with staring hideous eyes.'

The phantom huntsmen were an old Saxon legend which goes back into the mists and myths of European folklore. Herne's story has been told and retold for over a thousand years, and still his ghost appears, wearing the antlers of a stag, riding a phantom black stallion, at the head of a pack of baying black hounds. Legend has it that he appears to warn of times of trouble, and gallops through Windsor Great Park, only to disappear into thin air.

Herne was a young huntsman in the service of Richard II, King of England from 1377 to 1399, when he was deposed by Henry IV, the son of Hungerford's most famous benefactor, John O'Gaunt.

Like most of the aristocracy, Richard's favourite occupation was hunting, and he kept professional hunters to make sure of consistently good sport. Herne was a particularly gifted woodsman and was a favourite of the king, who always chose him to join his hunting party. Herne rode a beautiful black horse and was accompanied by two black hunting hounds. They were a good team, and the other keepers did not conceal their envy.

One day, Herne led the hunters on the track of a large

stag with a spectacular set of antlers. The animal took to its heels, and the king and Herne galloped after it. As Richard was riding hard behind the fleeing stag, the animal turned to gore him. Herne saw in an instant the danger to his royal master, and flung himself in the path of the charging stag. He thrust his dagger into the animal's neck and the king was saved. Herne was badly wounded, and the stag lay dying from Herne's dagger thrust.

The king was deeply shocked, and called for the hunting party to dismount to see what they could do for his injured huntsman. Richard did not want to lose the man who had served him so well, and offered a large reward to anyone who could save him. The other hunstmen, secretly pleased that this young upstart had got his come-uppance, merely suggested putting him out of his misery.

At that point, a mysterious figure appeared and told the king he was Philip Urswick, a physician, and that Herne would die if he was not treated immediately. The hunting party looked at the newcomer with deep suspicion. The king asked him if he was a poacher, and the huntsmen promptly claimed that he must be, as no one had ever seen him before. But the man was well dressed and was riding a fine horse, so Richard decided his only option was to give Urswick a chance.

The stranger took out a large hunting knife and set about cutting the antlers from the dead stag. He removed them and, to everyone's surprise, placed them on Herne's head. Then he ordered the huntsmen to make a stretcher out of branches and carry Herne to his hut in the forest. He told them his patient would recover under his care, and would be back at the king's side in one month's time.

The keepers were not pleased. The chance of getting rid of their rival was slipping away and they rounded on Urswick. He asked them what they could do for him if he took their part, but they were poor men and had nothing to offer him. The wily Urswick told them his prophecy would come true, but that he would cast a spell which would cause Herne to lose his mastery of woodcraft. In return, the keepers would perform the first task Urswick asked of them.

Urswick proved right, and a month later, the fully recovered Herne was provided with rooms at Windsor Castle. The king, delighted with his swift recovery, gave him a silver hunting horn and a purse of gold.

But Herne had lost his touch, and was now a failure on the hunt. His former magic had left him, and the king soon became irritated with Herne's inability to provide a good day's sport. He was dismissed, much to the delight of the jealous keepers. The distraught Herne, robbed of the only life he knew or wanted, rode off in a mad gallop into the forest, wearing the antlers which Urswick had used to save his life. Later that day, his lifeless body was found. He had hanged himself on an oak tree.

The man who found him went to the castle for help, and returned with the keepers of the forest. But when they got to the tree, the body was gone. A storm was brewing, and as they wondered what to do, a bolt of lightning split the tree almost in half.

The curse of Herne was then transferred to the other keepers. King Richard was mightily displeased with their lack of results on hunting trips, and the keepers felt the lash of the royal tongue. They decided to consult Urswick again. He told them to go to Herne's Oak, as it quickly and permanently became known, and follow whatever instructions they received.

The unhappy band arrived at midnight to find the ghost of Herne, wearing his antlers. He ordered them to return the next night with horses and hounds, ready for the hunt. They duly complied, and Herne galloped off at their head. Deep in the forest, the hunting party stopped and Urswick appeared, as if by magic.

Urswick greeted the hunters and reminded them of their promise to him. Now was the moment of truth, when they must pay the price for their wicked jealousy, and for Urswick's collaboration with their dastardly plot.

He commanded them to follow Herne to the ends of the earth. They would become his hunting party, condemned to follow him, night after night, slaughtering the deer of the forest. Mesmerised, they did as they were bid, and soon the tale came to the ear of the king, who was told of the strange night-time zombies who were depleting the royal forests at an alarming rate.

Richard called the head keeper to him to demand an explanation. The poor man was terrified out of his wits. What the keepers had initially seen as a bit of strange magic which had turned to their advantage had backfired badly on them, and they were now slaves to some dark force which they had no option but to obey. The frightened keeper blurted out the truth to the king, expecting the royal wrath to be swift and unmerciful.

But Richard thought carefully before taking action, and consulted his Queen, Anne of Bohemia, whose upbringing was steeped in the magical forests around her home in Prague. Herne had saved his life, and Richard, in good faith, had allowed the mysterious Urswick to become involved. Richard concluded that Herne could justifiably claim that he had been wronged, and commanded the keepers to take him with them on the next night's hunt.

Midnight came, and the king rode at the head of his keepers to where Herne's Oak stood with its coat of mistletoe. The ghost of Herne was silent, astride his black horse, with his two black hounds at his feet. King Richard approached, and asked Herne why he was acting in such a violent and destructive way. Herne replied that he was entitled to his revenge for such bad treatment at the hands of his fellow keepers. They were responsible for his death, and now he would be responsible for theirs. He told the king they must be hanged from Herne's Oak, or the dreadful hauntings would continue as long as King Richard reigned. Then the ghost of Herne disappeared.

Richard returned thoughtfully to the castle, pondering his response to Herne's demand. He was not disposed to lose his entire band of keepers, but could see no alternative. The next day he had every one of them hanged on the oak tree, exactly as Herne had commanded.

Herne's Oak was accidentally cut down in 1796, on the confused orders of George III. In 1863 Queen Victoria planted a replacement, unfortunately in the wrong place. Her son, Edward VII, planted another oak on the original site in 1906, which still stands in the private section of Home Park. The timber of the original oak became highly prized, and was used for making an astonishing variety of artifacts, from furniture to tea caddies.

Herne never troubled King Richard again, and the king once more returned to his favourite forest pursuit. The Herne problem soon paled into insignificance, and Richard found himself fighting for his life to put down a succession of uprisings by peasants, unruly barons, and last of all, by his cousin Duke Henry of Lancaster, son of John O'Gaunt. Henry's rebellion overwhelmed Richard, and Henry IV was declared king in 1399. Richard died within the year, reputedly murdered at Pontefract Castle.

Herne's ghost had kept his promise to Richard, but now he was back. The spectral hunt, exactly as described in the Anglo Saxon Chronicle all those years before, returned to plague the countryside and terrify the people.

So how was it that the chronicle described Herne over 250 years before the events took place? The answer is that Herne's story had already been legend for at least a millenium, and was firmly lodged in the superstitious minds of the people of the Dark and Middle Ages. The first reference to Herne which names him specifically is in William Shakespeare's *Merry Wives of Windsor*, written in 1597. The character of Mistress Page describes Herne thus:-

'There is an old tale goes that Herne the Hunter,
Sometime a keeper here in Windsor Forest,
Doth all the winter time, at still midnight,
Walk around about an oak, with great ragg'd horns;
And there he blasts the tree, and takes the cattle,
And makes milch-kine yield blood, and shakes a chain
In a most hideous and dreadful manner.
You have heard of such a spirit, and well you know

53

The superstitious idle-headed eld
Received, and did deliver to our age,
This tale of Herne the Hunter for a truth.'

But this was not Herne's first incarnation. He, or some similar spirit, was well known in the religious myths of pre-history. Horned gods had been revered as symbols of strength and virility since time immemorial. There are still remote tribes who have this allegiance today, and deer antlers were until this century commonly used as head-dresses by peoples who relied on hunting, such as North American Indians and Eskimos.

The oak tree was similarly revered, and is even mentioned in the Old Testament as where pagan worshippers conducted their religious ceremonies. It is ironic, and worthy of note, that Berkshire's county coat of arms consists of a stag and an oak tree. The most striking parallel to Herne is told in the stories of Norse and Saxon legends.

Four of our days of the week are named after the gods of these legends. Friday commemorates Frey, the Norse weather god. Thursday is named after Thor, Norse god of thunder, and Tuesday after Tiw, the ancient Saxon god of war. Wednesday is Woden's day, named after the chief god of the Saxon pagans. His name was known all over northern Europe, and was pronounced differently everywhere, although most people knew him as Woden or Odin.

One of the mainstays of the religion of these pre-Christian people was the cycle of the four seasons. Death and regeneration were quite natural to them, and they quite happily applied the principle to their gods. Thus, Woden replaced Tiw as 'Old Sky Father' and chief of the gods, and was himself later recycled to become the god of the homeless dead, leading a multitude of lost souls on a spectral hunt, all through the winter months.

Woden led the hunt on his eight-legged horse, Sleipnir, and regenerated himself by being hung on an oak tree, which meant he also became known as 'The Gallows God'. Warriors captured in battle were often hanged as a sacrifice to Woden, and the Norsemen believed that to die honourably in battle would give them entrance to Valhalla, the Nordic version of heaven, where they would spend eternity, feasting and fighting.

The legend of Woden's 'Wild Hunt' was common to most of the peoples of northern Europe, and the story of him being hanged on the tree, only to rise again, holds a very close parallel to the death of Christ on the cross. But although the early Christian missionaries fully exploited the similarities between their faith and that of their converts, the basic pagan belief in the power of the weather and the seasons was discouraged by the Church of Rome. The Church was in business as a broker to salvation, and beliefs over which it had no control could be prejudicial to its fees and tariffs. Competition was bad for business, and the deal was that guaranteed eternal life was bought at the price of exclusive loyalty to Mother Church.

But it never succeeded in entirely stamping out these ancient beliefs, and many of them are still manifested today. The Saxons believed you were safe from the Wild Hunt if you put a stag's antlers on your house. There are still antlers on houses today. We may no longer believe in goblins and evil spirits; but just watch a child's face fall if you say there is no such thing as the tooth fairy.

So, it seems Herne the Hunter is the most recent embodiment of the wild hunter at the head of his forlorn army of lost souls, galloping across the countryside in deep midwinter. His appearance supposedly presages disaster of some sort, and he was certainly seen 13 years after his master King Richard died after losing his throne to Henry IV. Herne sallied forth the night before King Henry died. He has been seen many times thereafter by all sorts of people, portending disasters large and small. He appeared just before the French Revolution, before the Great Depression of the 1930s, the abdication of Edward VIII, and to warn of the outbreak of World War II in 1939. He and the hunt have been seen countless times by a myriad individuals. The ghost of a dog is said to appear near Maidenhead Thicket when

Herne rides out. Known as 'The White Dog of Feens', its melancholy howling indicates that Herne is on his way.

But Herne really belongs to Windsor, and that is where he likes to be. In 1976, a young soldier was on guard duty at the castle, having drawn the unpopular duty of being the lone sentry on watch in a remote part of the estate. Standing at the ready with his rifle, the sentry watched in amazement as a statue seemed to come to life before him. There, clearly visible, was Herne the Hunter, dressed in deerskins and wearing the antlers of a stag. The sentry fainted, and was found later by another soldier.

Castle guards have reported sightings of Herne over many years, and seem almost to expect him to put in an appearance. One sentry in Victorian times was so jumpy that he almost shot the Dean of Windsor. It was a cold winter's night, and the kind-hearted clergyman was walking down to the sentry-box to take the man a hot drink. When the sentry heard footsteps and saw a figure in a long black cloak walking towards him, he lost his nerve and fired his carbine, missing the Dean by inches. The kindly Dean would have said nothing, but the sound of the shot meant the guard was called out, and the sentry had to give an account of himself. His punishment was 20 lashes; and he promised himself he would never see Herne again as long as he lived.

11

Wild Will Darrell of Littlecote

O LD Mother Barnes shivered by the kitchen fire of her tiny cottage at Great Shefford on the Lambourn Downs. The wind howled through the shutters, and the driving rain forced the mangy dog in the yard to seek shelter in the tumbledown barn.

It was the year of Our Lord 1575, and the Widow Barnes was the village midwife. It was late at night, and she was tired. She bolted the kitchen door – then stood back in alarm as a series of heavy blows nearly took it off its hinges.

'Who's there?' asked the frightened widow.

A gruff voice replied that she was needed urgently to deliver a baby. She had no choice but to open the door to the two scruffy ruffians standing outside. Both carried crude matchlock pistols in their belts. One was holding the reins of two waiting horses. They told her she would be blindfolded and taken to a nearby great house to ease the birth of a child to a woman of noble birth. They promised she would not be harmed, but would be well rewarded if a good job was done.

The taller of the two men lifted her up behind him on his horse, and the trio set out in the rain across the pitch black countryside, with the widow hanging on grimly as the two horses went as fast as their riders dared.

She was helped from the saddle, and felt herself being led through a great door, which closed with a hollow thud behind her. The two servants were left in the hall, and Mother Barnes was led down the corridors and up the stairs of what was obviously a very large house.

Although still blindfolded, the widow had the presence of mind to count the steps she took in the passageways and on the stairs on her way to the room where she was to deliver the child. There was only one house in the area big enough — it was Littlecote Manor, just outside Hungerford.

She felt the blindfold being removed, and blinked in the candlelight of a woman's bedroom. Before her was a nobleman. From his dress and demeanour, she could see he was the master of the house, Mr William Darrell. The Darrell family had acquired Littlecote in 1415 and were well known in the area. William was known as 'Wild Will' Darrell and was famous for his love of hunting.

He drew close to Mother Barnes and whispered in her ear. The widow took care to remember everything he said, and next day reported the whole story of what was to be a horrific event to local magistrate Anthony Bridges. He instructed his clerk to write it all down, and a transcript survives to this day.

Darrell said to her 'In yonder bed lyeth the gentlewoman; go unto her and see thou dost thy uttermost endevoyre towards her, and if she be safely delyvered, thou shalt not fayle of greate reward; but if she myscarrie in her traveyle, thou shalt die.'

The midwife got to work, but never saw the woman's face, which was covered with a mask. Her identity is not certain, but rumours that it was Darrell's sister are doubtful. It is more likely to have been Wild Will's mistress, Lady Anne of Hungerford. She was older than Darrell, and would have been much more likely than a younger woman to have perished in childbirth.

Old Mother Barnes delivered a boy child, and because there were no clothes for him, wrapped him in her apron. She carried the infant to the next room to ask Darrell for clothing. He was standing by a huge fireplace, awaiting her arrival.

He seized the child from the startled midwife's arms and hurled it into the fire. As she nearly fainted with horror, Darrell ground the pathetic bundle into the embers with his boot, and the baby was consumed by the flames. Stories abound of servants hearing the pathetic and ghostly cries of the murdered infant, and the floor next to the fireplace is said to run red with blood.

Darrell told Mother Barnes to see to the masked woman, who was now lying unconscious on her bed. The midwife did what she could to make sure the woman was comfortable, but was already planning her revenge. Very cautiously, she took her scissors to the curtains of the four-poster bed and cut away a piece of damask. She hid it in her bag, and stood stiff and silent as Darrell gave her a purse of coins and ordered her to be blindfolded. She counted the steps again on the way out, and was bundled onto the back of a horse. As she endured the long and uncomfortable ride home, she determined not to let the foul murderer escape his evil deed.

Before she retired to her bed that night, she cursed the Darrell family. No Darrell would ever inherit Littlecote Estate, or enjoy the fruits of its land. The curse has held true to this day.

Widow Barnes also decided to take civil as well as psychic action. She wanted Darrell brought to justice, and was determined to use every means at her disposal to that end. She went to see a well respected local magistrate to make a deposition of what she had seen. Anthony Bridges, who also lived at Great Shefford, took down everything she said, and a copy of the document is still in the ownership of the Darrell family. What Mother Barnes did not know was that Bridges was Wild Will's cousin.

Even so, the curse started to work. Widow Barnes told the authorities she had counted the steps at the Littlecote staircase, and produced the piece of cloth she had cut from the bed-curtains. Darrell was arrested and brought before Salisbury Assizes to be tried by Judge John Popham the Attorney General, who became Lord Chief Justice in 1592.

But Darrell had bribed the judge, by offering him the inheritance of Littlecote upon his death. The jury was said to be convinced of Darrell's guilt, but Judge Popham directed them to acquit him. Darrell walked free from the court, but only to demonstrate that Mother Barnes' curse had hit home. Popham would now be master of Littlecote, and the Darrell family would never inherit. Wild Will made over the reversion to Popham in 1586.

A letter was discovered at Longleat in about 1879 from Sir H. Knyvett, of Chilton Foliat, to Sir John Thynne, of Longleat, dated 2nd January 1579, soon after the baby incident. Residing at Longleat was a Mr Bonham, whose sister was supposed to be living with Darrell as his mistress. Kynvett's letter asks that Bonham enquire of his sister as to the welfare of her children, how many there were and what became of them, 'For that the report of the murder of one of them was increasing foully, and would touch Will Darrell to the quick'.

In 1583 Darrell offered Lord Chancellor Bromley the then huge sum of £5,000 'to be his good friend'. It is not known if the bribe was accepted.

Wild Will did not enjoy his dearly bought freedom for very long. Justice from a higher court was meted out to him; his passion for the chase was the quirk of fate which was his undoing. While out on the estate, he rode his big black horse hard at a stile in pursuit of a deer. As the stallion leapt at the fence, an infant engulfed in a ball of flame appeared before him. The terrified horse shied and Darrell was thrown violently to the ground. His neck was broken and he died a painful death.

Judge John Popham took possession of Littlecote. He was knighted in 1592 and continued a distinguished legal career, which saw him as a judge in the trials of Sir Walter Raleigh and the infamous Guy Fawkes. Sir John died peacefully in 1607. Littlecote was to remain in his family until 1929. His portrait, great chair and the thumbscrews he used to extract confessions from reluctant prisoners are still in the Great Hall there.

Wild Will's ghost is reputed to haunt the park, particularly the place known as 'Darrell's Stile'. Legend has it that on dark nights Wild Will rides out at full gallop on his huge black horse, its nostrils flared, breath like steam and its eyes burning like coals. The legend also crops up in old Saxon mythology, with the god Woden riding his very similar black horse. This part of the country was settled by the Saxons after the Romans left, and even as late as William the Conqueror, there was a Saxon bishop at nearby Ramsbury.

Near Darrell's Stile was a muddy pond. Mr Ted Hunt was born and brought up nearby, and remembers the fear and nausea he felt whenever he went near it as a boy. He never saw Wild Will, but he learned to fear him. Mr Hunt is now retired, but remembers coming home on leave from the army in 1940 as an 18 year old soldier, walking past the pond on his way home.

'Suddenly, I felt something pulling at me, towards the pond,' he said. 'I looked behind me, but there was nothing there. Still I felt this power drawing me towards the pond. I turned and ran as fast as I could. I've never liked walking past there.'

'My sister Alice worked as a maid at the house,' he said. 'One day, she was alone, working upstairs near the fireplace where the baby was murdered. There was no one else in that part of the house, and she distinctly heard a baby crying.'

Darrell's Stile and the pond disappeared in 1941, along with Darrell's Elm, which grew in the park only 100 metres from the main door of the house. The tree also came to feature in the legend, and it was said that Littlecote would prosper as long as the tree flourished. Somebody must have believed it, because for many years the old elm was supported by iron posts and chains.

But when war broke out in 1939, the War Ministry desperately needed airfields, and the stile and pond disappeared under the concrete runway of Ramsbury airfield, which was briefly taken over by the Royal Air Force. King George VI and Queen Elizabeth – now the Queen Mother – had visited Littlecote in 1941, then in 1943 the RAF handed the airfield over to the USAAF 437 Troop Carrier Group, and American paratroops took off from there in the Normandy landings and the liberation of Holland in 1944. Now the aerodrome has been largely returned to agriculture, but Wild Will's name lives on in the nearby Darrell's Farm and Darrell's Cottages.

The park was bought in 1985 by Mr Peter de Savary. By 1995, it was in the hands of the receiver, a sad fate for such a magnificent house.

What happened to Darrell's body after his death is something of a mystery. Some say the local churchmen refused to bury him in hallowed ground, others that he lies in the family vault at the Church of the Holy Cross in nearby Ramsbury. The Darrells certainly had a chapel there, and their tombs are still to be seen, although which is which is not known, because the parish records for that period have been lost. To add insult to injury, the church was looted by Roundhead soldiers in 1644, and they stole all the brass nameplates off the gravestones in the chapel.

Contemporary members of the Darrell family are unsure where Wild Will was finally laid to rest, but Mrs Catherine Astor of Inkpen says that her father, Sir Jeffrey Darrell, feels confident of the family chapel theory, and is supported by Sir Seton Wills, who lived for much of his life at Littlecote after inheriting it from his father.

There is a plaque in memory of Wild Will in St Mary's Church, Kintbury. It says 'In memory of Sir William Darrell, Knight, of Littlecote in the county of Wiltshire. Lived without issue and died October 1, 1588. Uncle of Sir John Darrell of West Woodhay, High Sheriff of Berkshire 1626, buried here May 14, 1637.' Sir John's uncle Will was not a knight, but he obviously felt obliged to stick up for him. Sir John is thought to have been responsible for the original building of West Woodhay House, ancestral home of the Henderson family.

Littlecote has a history stretching back to Roman times, and spectral sights and sounds have been recorded there for many years. It is little wonder that the Romans decided to settle there. The countryside is idyllic, and the villa and farm were next to the river Kennet, abundant with trout and other fish.

The floors of a Roman villa and farm were unearthed close to the manor house in the early eighteenth century.

Serious excavation did not start until 1977, with the arrival of archaeologist Bryn Walters.

'Littlecote is one of the spookiest places in Britain,' he said. 'There are enough spectral tales there to fill a book.' The house and stables abound with tales of faces appearing at windows, mysterious footsteps, doors opening and closing all on their own, figures walking through walls, eerie cries and moans, sudden drops in temperature and strange smells. Mr Walters recalled that the previous owners of the house, the Wills family, the famous Bristol tobacco merchants, were all familiar with the little quirks of the house. Sir Seton's grandfather, Sir Ernest Wills, was awakened one night, and thinking that burglars had got in, went to investigate.

He slipped quietly into the Long Gallery to see the ghost of a woman carrying a rush-light walking towards him through the darkness. It was by no means the first time Sir Ernest had seen this particular spectre, in fact it was a bit of an anti-climax for him. The ghostly figure must have been astonished when the irascible knight snorted that he would not have bothered to get out of bed if he had known it was only a ghost walking about. He turned on his heel and stamped off back to bed.

While Mr Walters and his band of volunteers were carefully excavating the extraordinary mosaics of the Roman buildings, Sir Seton allowed them to live in the old stables, which had been cleaned out and left quite unused for 25 years.

'It's the only complete Roman villa where the floors have been completely exposed in the whole of Britain,' said Mr Walters. 'It is a very important site, and running straight past it was a Roman military road.

'There is a long-established history of a ghostly Roman legion marching through the grounds of Littlecote. On two occasions, the volunteers staying at the stables were disturbed in the middle of the night by the crunch of marching feet and the sound of horses. Roman horses were covered in metal decorations, and the volunteers could clearly hear them jangling as they walked along. The noise started from the direction of Hungerford and faded away in the west towards Ramsbury, following the line of the Roman road on the south side of the Kennet river. The road has now disappeared almost completely, but was probably the original route from east to west across the country, forerunner of the A4 Bath Road. Also, I have been told other people have heard the sounds of men and horses crossing the lawns in front of the mansion. I think it very unlikely that these are Civil War ghosts. The Roman road had long since disappeared by that time.'

Mr Walters expressed his concern to Sir Seton Wills because volunteers were leaving the site in droves after ghostly encounters, particularly in the stable block. 'We never saw anything, but there would suddenly be the overpowering smell of horses – we could smell their sweat, urine, and the hay and straw made us sneeze. Sir Seton was astonished and told us there had been no horses there for 25 years.'

Mr Walters is justifiably proud of the excavations at Littlecote, which were financed by Sir Seton. The mosaic floors are among the finest examples. 'The place was originally a large farm, not that much different to a modern farm, with grain stores, silos and brewing tanks. The mosaic is very unusual, and dates from around AD 360, in the reign of the Emperor Julian. In my opinion, something dramatic must have happened. The farm was allowed to run down, and the buildings became a shrine to Bacchus. All the evidence indicates that the place became a sort of initiation centre into religious rites for the priests of Bacchus. It is still a very mysterious place.'

The cult of Bacchus, Roman god of wine and revelry, often associated with drunken orgies, almost eclipsed Christianity under the Emperor Julian, whose proper title was Flavius Claudius Julianus. He ruled Rome from AD 361 to 363, and renounced Christianity in favour of paganism – especially the cult of Bacchus.

Despite having to suffer the ghosts of Littlecote being

unleashed, Mr Walters is keen to continue with the excavation. 'I have an open mind about it,' he said. 'I have had some very unpleasant experiences, and some very amusing ones. There is a lot more work to be done at Littlecote. We haven't found the burial area yet, and there must be one there somewhere.' What more horrible secrets could be unearthed at Littlecote – which is already one of the most haunted houses in the country?

Today, the great house is looked after by caretaker John Tripp. He knows every inch of its fabric, and does not worry about the old gentleman with the dog who walks up the staircase at the back of the house and then suddenly disappears. The only thing that really annoys him is when some ghostly hand moves the Civil War armour in the Great Hall, often changing the position of one of the ancient iron helmets on display. It's not the spooky pranks that he minds – it's the fact that they set off the burglar alarm. But he is philosophical about it. 'All ghosts fade with time,' he said.

12

The Wargrave Joker

THE story of Lord Barrymore's life is like a fairy tale, and his gory and untimely death are worthy of any self respecting ghost. His mischievous spirit still haunts the house he built, and which still stands today in Wargrave High Street.

Richard, Earl of Barrymore, Viscount Buttevant and Baron Perry was born to the Irish peerage in 1769, and succeeded to his title at the age of four. When he was six years old, he was sent to England to be educated. He stayed with the family of Rev John Tickell at Wargrave Hall until the age of 14, after which he went to Eton, in the best tradition of the upper classes.

Young Barrymore led a charmed life. His aunt, the Countess of Huntingdon, promised him some 'pocket money', and duly sent him £1,000 – more money than most men would see in their lifetime in those days. The teenage lord set about seriously enjoying himself, starting at the races. Before he had turned 15, he was a regular punter at Newmarket and other racecourses, and he was not frightened to bet large sums on any horse he fancied.

Lady Huntingdon died while Barrymore was still a pupil at Eton, and the unpleasant task of informing the boy fell to the headmaster. Barrymore was in a Latin class, engrossed in the study of Virgil's writings. The head tried to break it to him gently.

'I am sorry to inform you that your aunt is ill,' he said, with the utmost diplomacy.

'I am sorry to hear it,' replied Barrymore, without looking up from his books.

'She is very ill indeed, my Lord.'

'Thank you,' said Barrymore.

The head cleared his throat and said 'My Lord, she is dying.'

'Dying?' asked the boy in astonishment. 'Come, come, Headmaster.'

The head completely lost his composure. 'She is dead, my Lord. Now you know the worst, go and make the best of an irretrievable misfortune.'

Barrymore licked his pencil and went back to his Virgil.

He was a great prankster. He and his friends thought nothing of sneaking out at midnight in the summer holidays and swapping round all the local pub signs. But because of his wealth, the local citizenry put up with him, despite often being the butt of his merry japes.

By the time he left Eton, he was one of the country's leading experts on horse racing, and was famous for his ability to spot a winner in the making. He was a steward at the racecourse in Reading, had a string of horses of his own and won and lost thousands of pounds on the sport of kings, with his jockeys dressed in his distinctive blue and yellow colours. He had his own pack of hounds and hunted regularly. His four black servants, who wore a livery of scarlet and silver, accompanied him when he rode to hounds, and sounded directions on a quartet of French horns. Barrymore was anti-slavery, and treated his servants very well. An accomplished musician, he was famous for impromptu improvisation on any instrument. He loved founding clubs for the enjoyment of himself and others, and the best known was 'The Bacchanalian Society', which was probably a fair reflection of his attitude.

He also took an interest in boxing, which was a much bloodier sport in those days, with many of the protagonists being killed or seriously injured in fights for large purses, with a lot of gambling money riding on the winner. Barrymore attended hundreds of bare-knuckle bouts, and sponsored a boxer of his own, Tom 'Tinman' Hooper, a prize fighter from Bristol. Barrymore brought him to

Wargrave to live at the fine house he had built out of an old cottage, next door to his childhood home of Wargrave Hall, to which he had returned after leaving Eton. Although he rented Barrymore House, he spent a fortune transforming it from a medium sized cottage into an elegant residence.

By the age of 20, he was the epitome of the young buck, and was well known in court circles. By now, the young lord had acquired a fascination for the theatre. It was a golden age of entertainment in London, with new plays, new writers and new theatres for actors to perform, with no expense spared.

The playwright Richard Brinsley Sheridan was busy writing a string of comedies which delighted the sophisticated tastes of London society. *The Rivals*, *The Critic* and *School for Scandal* and others were tremendously successful, and are still performed to this day. It was the age of David Garrick, who made acting into a glamorous profession, of William Wordsworth, and later of Sir Walter Scott, Jane Austen and of Beau Brummell, who came from Newbury and was probably the world's greatest dandy.

Barrymore was not content just to enjoy the theatre in London. He wanted one of his own, and set about designing a grandiose building to house over 700 people, all in great style and comfort, with the most up to date technology at his disposal. All of this was happening in a riverside village of less than 1,500 people, many of whom were illiterate.

The first play to be acted at the theatre was in September 1791. It was a comedy version of *Robinson Crusoe*, and the whole production cost £60,000. Soon after came *The Marriage of Figaro*, with the cast including both Barrymore and the Hon Lucius Cary, a descendant of Lord Falkland, the distinguished Royalist general of the Civil War. Barrymore had no difficulty in persuading his aristocratic friends to play small parts in these productions. In the intervals, servants dressed in scarlet and gold livery would serve tea, coffee, chocolate, and orange or lemon juice. They would leave bottles of wine buried in the garden for guests to find in a treasure hunt after the performance. The actors would often get riotously drunk on champagne.

For his 21st birthday, he organised a grand masked ball. London society turned out in force for what they all knew would be a huge extravaganza for Barrymore's coming of age. The Prince Regent, later George IV, was there, along with a small army of minor royalty, with Lord Craven and the German Margravine of Anspach making the journey from their homes at Hamstead Marshall.

Despite, or perhaps because of, the pedigree of his guests, Barrymore employed one of his team of boxers as a liveried doorman. He was known as 'Big Ben', and there was no trouble with gatecrashers. The vicar of Wargrave was not invited to the festivities, but tried to use his position to get in. He was a brave man indeed to argue, but was politely informed that as he had no invitation the doorman had instructions to eject him. He was courteously but firmly escorted to the door.

Barrymore was MP for Heytesbury, a village in Wiltshire, and nearly got himself elected for Reading. Two days before the polls closed, he put himself up, and scored a large share of the vote – but not large enough to get elected. The *Berkshire Mercury* of December 1788 records his immense popularity at the time. 'Lord Barrymore gave a fat beast to the people to have at Christmas,' it said. The following year, he endowed a trophy at Reading racecourse. It was the 50 guinea plate, and was highly prized.

As well as the theatre across the road from his home, Barrymore built accommodation for the actors, who were brought down from London by horse and carriage and lived in sumptuous style. But the theatre's existence was short lived. It had cost Barrymore £300,000, and he was now in severe financial trouble. Matters were made worse by his purchase of the London Theatre in Savile Row. The threat of bankruptcy seemed to be staved off for a time by his marriage, in 1792, to Caroline Goulding, with whom he is supposed to have galloped off to Gretna Green.

The marriage was even more short lived than the theatre. It is not known if Lady Barrymore ever bore him an heir, but it is true to say that a famous family of American actors adopted the name Barrymore. Mr Herbert Blythe, who was born in 1847, changed his name to Maurice Barrymore, and was the father of Lionel Barrymore, born in 1878, Ethel, born in 1879, and John, born in 1882. After being married only eight months, Barrymore was called upon for military service. The French revolutionary government was running out of aristocrats to massacre on the guillotine, and had decided to attack Belgium and the Netherlands. Britain responded by sending an army against the French.

So it was that Barrymore found himself as a young army officer in Dover. He had volunteered for the Berkshire Militia to join one of his friends, Lord Craven, who held the rank of major. The Craven family lived in grand style on a huge estate at Hamstead Marshall, and has suffered for centuries under a gypsy curse which claims the life of the first born son of every generation. Simon, the last Earl of Craven, was killed in a mysterious car accident in Eastbourne, leaving his infant son to grow up under the shadow of the curse.

At the age of 23 Barrymore was guarding French prisoners of war when he met the grim reaper in a most bizarre fashion. His musket went off in his face and he was killed instantly.

His creditors descended like a pack of vultures, for despite his marriage, Barrymore died penniless, and heavily in debt. The grand theatre at Wargrave was the only thing they could get their hands on, and they ripped it to pieces. Today, there is not a trace of it, although the new houses built there are appropriately called 'Barrymore Stables', and are just round the corner from 'Garrick Mews'.

Barrymore House still stands in the High Street – with just a trace of ghostly perfume, occasionally, at the top of the stairs.

Mr John French lived for 15 years at Barrymore House and was often puzzled by strange happenings. He often saw the ghost of a woman wearing a grey silk dress.

'Her dress made a shushing noise as she walked through

the house, and we could smell her lavender perfume,' he said. 'Lavender was popular about 100 years ago, and it was grown commercially in Wargrave. If we tried to follow her, she would promptly disappear. I have no idea who she was.'

Barrymore House was rarely locked in the days that Mr French lived there, because the keys were wont to mysteriously disappear. 'All the doors had the sort of keys you would expect for a large old house,' he said. 'We would leave keys in keyholes, and they would just disappear. After about a year, we would find them in a pile on the bedroom floor. We never discovered why.'

Another phenomenon was the unseen force which tried to push the two male members of the household downstairs. Mr French and his son experienced this on numerous occasions, but brushed it off as a laugh. Could it have been Barrymore, master of the practical joke? Mr French doesn't know.

'It got quite spooky at times, especially when I was working at home late at night. I would have the dog at my feet, and he often seemed to see something. He would track it with his eyes and his hackles would come up. He would never go up to the top floor of the house. Up there was a bedroom which had seven crucifixes on the walls. Under the floorboards we found a wooden Bible cover dated 1660. It was hand painted and made in Italy, but we never found out who left it there.'

The partly Tudor house is right by the river Thames and still has its original timbers, marked with an arrowhead, which shows they were originally ship's timbers, taken from a large man o'war at the end of its service. Was it the ghosts that caused Mr French to sell up and move out?

'We never worried about that kind of thing, and after a few years, the ghosts went away,' he said.

Mr French said several accounts of Barrymore's story were written soon after his death. 'He had both friends and enemies, and how you perceive him depends on which account you believe. I think Barrymore was a cocky, stuck up Jack-the-lad, who went bankrupt for over £1 million, which was a fantastic sum in those days, probably equivalent to a billion now.'

Some of the doubts about the story of Barrymore's life must be laid at the door of his friend and personal biographer, John Williams. He was a professional hack, and tailored his stories as the inclination took him. He wrote under the pen name of Anthony Pasquin, and although Barrymore was a good friend to him, Williams was certainly on the receiving end of many of Barrymore's practical jokes.

One such which amused Barrymore and frightened Williams to death was when Barrymore sent his servants out to buy a coffin. He then put one of them in it, theatrically made up to look like a cadaver, with instructions to play dead. The coffin and its macabre contents were delivered to the door of the intended victim and left standing bolt upright on the doorstep. The gang would then ring the doorbell and retire swiftly. The shock of opening the front door to a corpse in a coffin was too much for the servants of many households, and they promptly fainted, at which Barrymore fell about laughing.

On the day he died, Barrymore and his platoon of soldiers were escorting 16 French prisoners of war near Dover. Barrymore had got bored and was taking pot shots at the seagulls with his musket. John French, who lived alongside Barrymore's ghost for so many years, has studied accounts of Barrymore's death and considers any theory that he committed suicide to be unlikely. Mr French is a former artillery officer and keen student of the Napoleonic wars. He has considerable knowledge of the weapons available at that time.

'He was almost certainly using a flintlock military musket belonging to one of his men. That type of weapon could be loaded and fired quite quickly if you were prepared to take a chance. The powder was tipped down the barrel from a powder horn, which delivered the correct amount automatically. The soldier would then spit the ball down the barrel, and tap the butt on the ground instead of tamping down with the ramrod. It was known as 'tap loading', and avoided the need to prime the firing pan with powder. It was highly dangerous, and if the gun had a faulty firing lock, it would go off prematurely. The penalty for getting it wrong was that the weapon would go off in your face. Barrymore was certainly the sort of impatient man who would want to get as many shots at the gulls as possible. He was also careless, and I feel sure that he paid the price for his carelessness.'

After Barrymore's death, his body was taken away and hidden, for fear creditors might attempt to seize it for ransom from any family or friends sufficiently grieved to pay up. It was taken secretly to Wargrave and buried on Sunday, 17th February 1793, in an unmarked grave in the chancel at Wargrave church. It remained unmarked because it was considered that some of the creditors were not above digging up the body and holding it to ransom.

He had a mortgage to the king's bankers of £130,000, plus countless other debts. Since leaving Eton, he had squandered over £300,000 on trivial items, and after a short but eventful life was bankrupt for over £1 million. Perhaps he was looking forward to the peace and quiet of the next world, where he could enjoy his practical jokes to his soul's content.

13

The Hunt for the Grey Lady

THE ghosts of Hurley had been sleeping for centuries – until someone came along to dig them up. They rose up in silent vigil until they were given back their peace.

The cause of all this turmoil was the arrival in 1924 of Colonel C.N. Rivers-Moore, who was obsessed with archaeology in general, and the burial place of a medieval queen in particular. Queen Editha's ghost, the Grey Lady, was a familiar legend in the village and surrounding area. The riverside hamlet consists of a few houses and a church, just off the road from Maidenhead to Henley. The little road leading into the village stops at the river Thames. It is here that Ladye Place, named after the medieval priory dedicated to Our Lady, Mother of Christ, is situated. The colonel moved into the large Edwardian house with its 20 acres of grounds, and soon got the builders in.

In the 12th century, the site had been occupied by monks from a cell of the Benedictine Abbey of Westminster, and they had built the Priory of St Mary there. The buildings were destroyed by fire in the 16th century and were rebuilt, only to be knocked about and largely replaced in 1903. Col Rivers-Moore knew something of the history of the place, and the legend that it contained the tomb of Queen Editha, the sister of Edward the Confessor.

Edward was the last Anglo-Saxon king of England to die peacefully. He was succeeded by King Harold, who was defeated by Edward's cousin, Duke William of Normandy at the Battle of Hastings in 1066. Edward was a highly religious man, not really very interested in being king, and had spent years as a monk in Normandy during the period when the

Danish King Canute was on the English throne. He was the founder of Westminster Abbey, which he dedicated to St Peter, and had his palace at Westminster, which in those days was well outside London's city limits. Edward and Editha were regarded as saints, and he was canonised in 1161.

Obsessed with the legend of the Grey Lady, Col Rivers-Moore set about trying to find her burial place. Unusual circumstances triggered off the hunt that was to see a ten year search for Editha's tomb. A visitor claimed to have seen the ghost of a monk in a brown habit in the dining room, and said the ghost had told him that the fireplace should be removed. This was done, and behind the rather indifferent dining room fireplace was found a much more handsome one, dating from the 17th century.

The ghostly monk returned and was seen by other people. More monks materialised and it became common to see them walking in the cloisters with their arms folded and with cowls over their heads.

Col Rivers-Moore, far from being frightened at the hauntings, was impressed, and determined to find a way to communicate with the dead monks to discover the whereabouts of the Grey Lady's grave. Seances were held, and the excavations continued under the direction of the monkish phantoms, who appeared to be willing to help, and periodically issued ghostly instructions.

The first thing to be found was an ancient well, long disused. Old fireplaces and a host of objects were discovered, and the foundations of the old priory were laid bare. But Editha's last resting place was never located, and the colonel finally had to admit defeat.

The house was restored to some semblance of tidiness, and was sold in 1944. When the colonel left, so did the monks, and peace returned to Ladye Place. Even the Grey Lady herself was seen no more. One thing that interested visitors were not told was that Col Rivers-Moore was a gifted amateur magician and an expert at sleight of hand. His seances, complete with moving objects and turning tables, may or may not have been genuine. But the place was certainly steeped in history to the extent that so much disturbance was likely to waken the monkish ghosts. Whether they really gave advice on where to dig, we shall never know; but in a place so packed with medieval remains it would have been almost impossible not to find something, although the Grey Lady remained elusive to the last.

14

The Ghosts of Purley Hall

M ISS Emma Elizabeth Thoyts stayed at the hall over 100 years ago and felt a supernatural force. Miss Thoyts lived in rural splendour at Sulhamstead House, surrounded by acres of parkland. Sulhamstead House is now the headquarters training centre for the Thames Valley Police.

Writing in 1892, Miss Thoyts complained not only of the feeling of such a force but also of the terrible smell that went with it. She said 'In 1889, I was asked to stay there to be present at a meeting of the Berkshire Archaeological Society. When shown my room, I was nearly poisoned by the smell. It was late, and I began to undress when a panic urged me that the room was haunted. It was without rhyme or reason, but so positive that although I only had a vague idea where my hostess's room was, I resolved to go and seek her.'

'I knocked at the door I believed to be hers, and heard a voice say "come in", and gladly I entered. She persuaded me to return to my room, but on going there, the smell was so bad that I could not remain. I therefore shared her room for the night.

'Next day, I asked Miss Currie, Mrs Wilder's sister, if the room was haunted, and she said yes, that stories were told that cries were heard, and that a little child came and stared as one knelt at prayers.

'One of the girls of the Hawes family was very lovely; but was destroyed by her lover, a colonel in the army. In that room, her child was born – and murdered; the body being concealed in a cupboard. The cries are from the baby, answered by low moans from the wretched mother.

'When the room was whitewashed in 1890, a blocked up

window was found where the cupboard had been, showing that this and the next room were once all in one and were probably the drawing room. Nothing was found in the window.

'Of the Hawes family, little is known, except that they bought the property from the Hydes and changed the name from Hydes Hall to Purley Hall. They lost a lot of money in the South Sea Speculations, and only managed to keep the house by letting it to a tenant.

'In 1770 it was bought by Dr Wilder of Nunhide from Francis Hawes, a linen draper of Cheapside. Of the woman-kind of the Hawes family, nothing is known, but in Purley church is a tablet to Elizabeth Hawes.

'I was there when someone asked Mrs Wilder "Is not Purley haunted?" Mrs Wilder did not like that at all; and they hastily dropped the subject.'

It seems that one of the Hawes family's tenants at Purley was Warren Hastings, the first Governor-General of India, and he returned to live there for some years after Dr Wilder bought the property. Like so many others in the world of politics, Hastings had made enemies, and in 1788 was impeached in the House of Commons. He retired to Purley to put together his defence against accusations that could have sent him to the scaffold, and after a lengthy trial, was acquitted. He died a vindicated man at the age of 86.

Hastings' ghost was seen often in the house, which had acquired such an oppressive atmosphere that the people who lived there in the 1960s arranged a service of exorcism. They were delighted with its success, and reported that the atmosphere had changed completely, and although Hastings' ghost was still seen, it left a friendly and happy impression.

15

The Bere Court Treasure

BERE Court House near Pangbourne is reputed to be built on land which belonged to Reading Abbey. Over a century ago, a treasure trove of solid silver plates and dishes was found hidden in a secret room, its doors locked for centuries against prying eyes and greedy hands. No sightings are reported of the monks who lived here, but the ghost of a lady dressed in blue has been seen.

It was from this monastic house that the last Abbot of Reading was dragged to his death in 1539. Abbot Hugh Faringdon had refused to hand over Reading Abbey to King Henry VIII, who was greedy and impatient to get his hands on the treasure it contained. The abbot was attainted of high treason and locked up in the Tower of London while Henry's men drew up an inventory of everything the abbey contained, including saintly relics, gold and silver plate, tapestries, statues; anything of value which could be sold immediately.

Abbot Hugh was brought from London back to Reading for trial, and condemned to be hung, drawn and quartered. The sentence was carried out in front of the very abbey gateway where he had once given audience to the townspeople and led prayers for King Henry.

Bere Court was one of several grand houses visited by the redoubtable Miss Emma Elizabeth Thoyts of Sulhamstead, and she gave an account of it in her journal of 1892.

'All sorts of stories are told of the place, which is a gloomy red brick house, buried in a hollow in the hills. This old house is said to have been the hunting lodge and summer residence of the Abbots of Reading. It is from here that the

King's commissioners are said to have taken the last abbot to his trial and doom.

'The best bedroom is said to be haunted by a lady in blue; who she is is not clear. In the same room is a panel, and it is said that a dinner service was hidden behind it. Mr Finch, the clergyman at Pangbourne, told me that years ago, when a certain Mr Edward Clarke rented the house, he found, in a lumber room, a box too heavy to move. On writing to the owner, Mr Breedon, he obtained permission to open it. A whole service of silver plate was found and taken into use. After Mr Clarke's death, this plate disappeared, and has never since been heard of. The Breedons were longing to remove the panel when the house was dismantled in 1890. They did, but there was only a brick wall behind it.

'A piece of coloured fresco work could be seen through a broken panel over the mantelpiece. The caretaker told me it was one of the monks' altars.'

Whether Miss Thoyts managed to trace the hoard of silver she does not record, and it seems likely that it was either never seen again, or was spirited away by some unscrupulous soul for a quick financial reward. Such is the fate of so much of our heritage.

16

The Royal Ghosts of Windsor

IT would be surprising if there were no reports of things going bump in the night at Windsor Castle. The kings and queens of England have made the castle their home for over nine centuries, and have left their mark stamped indelibly on the ancient stones.

The castle has at least four royal ghosts, and legions of minor ones. Henry VIII can be heard wheezing and spluttering, Elizabeth I haunts the library, Charles I has been seen in the castle grounds, and lonely old George III still taps on the window to attract people's attention.

Henry VIII came to the throne a very popular king. As the young 'bluff Prince Hal', he was an energetic sportsman who enjoyed life to the full. Unfortunately, he didn't know when to stop, and did everything to excess. He was a ferocious glutton, and never stinted himself on wine, women and song. He had six wives and innumerable mistresses, and people who disagreed with him tended to come to a swift and sticky end.

His lifetime of self-indulgence took its toll, and in old age, Henry became grossly overweight, unfit and suffered from dropsy. His legs were badly ulcerated, and by the time he died in 1547, at the age of 56, he could barely drag himself unaided through the castle corridors. The king's spirit seems unwilling to leave the place he knew so well, and has been heard stumbling through the castle at dead of night.

The castle was also the favourite haunt of Elizabeth I, Henry's daughter. She loved Windsor and spent much of her time there, both dealing with matters of state, and retreating to the castle when life got too much for her. She was known to leave London on journeys to other parts of the kingdom, and not get any further than Windsor. She would send word ahead to her hosts that she was unable to journey beyond Windsor, which often left them somewhat irritated, as it was the custom to provide royalty with hospitality on a lavish scale, and country house owners would go to the expense of having another wing built, just to entertain the Virgin Queen. It is quite possible that some of the places which boast 'Queen Elizabeth I slept here' are unable to justify their claim, quite simply because Good Queen Bess got fed up on the journey and retired to Windsor.

She has appeared on a number of occasions. One of the most famous was in 1897, when she was seen by a young Grenadier Guards officer, Lieutenant Carr Glynn, in the castle library, almost 300 years after her death. He was reading in the library when he saw a woman walking across the floor towards him. In Queen Elizabeth's day, that part of the castle had been her royal apartments.

It was dusk on a winter's afternoon, and the woman was dressed in black, with a black lace scarf over her head and shoulders. He could hear her footsteps quite clearly as she approached him and could almost reach out and touch her as she walked past. He did not pay any particular attention, and assumed the woman had left the room by another exit. He was not familiar with the layout of the library, and saw the apparition glide up some steps into a small room which Elizabeth had built as a picture gallery. She was fond of walking through it and down a staircase onto the terrace. But the exit to the gallery had been blocked up years ago, and the staircase was long gone.

Lt Glynn looked up a few moments later when one of the castle servants entered the library, and asked who was the lady in black. The man said he had seen no one. Glynn rose from his chair and walked up the three steps to the gallery. Then he realised there was no doorway through which the apparition could have left the room. But she certainly wasn't there, and Lt Glynn again asked the servant who the dark lady was.

The man was clearly nervous, and was emphatic that nobody had entered the library while the lieutenant had been reading. After some questions, the servant told Glynn that the apparition had often been seen before, and was the ghost of Queen Elizabeth.

Lt Glynn's experience was reported to the librarian, Dr Holmes, who sent for the young subaltern and asked him to repeat his story. Glynn told him what he had seen. Dr Holmes listened intently and asked him to describe the apparition as closely as he was able. Glynn replied he had not taken that much notice, but he was an intelligent and observant man, and described her as best he could.

The librarian told the young soldier his description tallied with previous sightings of the queen, the most recent of which had been some years previously by Queen Victoria's daughter, also named Victoria, who after her marriage to the German Emperor became Empress Frederick III of Germany. As a child, she had seen Elizabeth's ghost in exactly the same place.

Queen Victoria was reputed to have taken enormous interest in the paranormal, and bygone rumour suggests she conducted seances in her private rooms at the castle, with her friend John Brown as medium. Victoria's beloved husband, Prince Albert of Saxe-Coburg-Gotha, had died in 1861 and she missed him terribly. There has been much speculation since about her relationship with Brown, who was a ghillie on her highland estate at Balmoral. He often accompanied her as she travelled round the country, and it seems she was happy to use his gifts as a medium to contact the ghost of Albert. The queen apparently kept records of these seances in a secret place, along with notes she had made about her relationship with Brown.

None of the queen's writings survived. Because of the possibility of them falling into the wrong hands, with an ensuing scandal that would rock the world at the height of the British Empire, Victoria was persuaded by the Dean of Windsor to destroy her notes about Brown. The notes on the seances she still kept hidden, but the dean found out where, and destroyed them immediately after her death. If there was any scandal about Queen Victoria, it went with her to the grave.

It would seem odd if Charles I did not make some sort of haunting protest. Charles Stuart came to the throne in 1625 and believed he possessed the divine right of kings, and that he was above the law. A lot of his subjects disagreed with this philosophy; the upshot being the Civil War which Charles and his aristocratic Cavalier army lost to the forces of Parliament.

Charles was imprisoned at Carisbrooke Castle on the Isle of Wight, and was brought to trial in London and beheaded in Whitehall in 1649. His body was brought to Windsor and the coffin placed on a table overnight. The next day, the corpse of Charles I of England was unceremoniously bundled away and buried beneath the vaults of St George's Chapel.

Charles was a very haughty and dignified man, and duly appears complete with his head. He has been seen in the castle and at the Canon's House, which is in the grounds. Those who have seen him say he is unmistakable, and looks exactly like the classical portraits of him painted during his lifetime.

One of Charles's ministers was the Duke of Buckingham, a wealthy and influential man, but a deeply unpopular one. Buckingham was the organiser of a series of costly and disastrous expeditions by British forces into Europe. Heavy taxation was levied to pay for them, and martial law was imposed, resulting in civilians being arbitrarily imprisoned without trial. No wonder the duke was unpopular.

The ghost of his father, Sir George Villiers, haunted Windsor Castle to try and warn his son against assassination. The story goes that Sir George appeared to a Guards officer and asked him to speak to the duke. The soldier thought it was a nightmare, and went back to sleep.

The ghost came again the next night, but the phlegmatic guardsman thought it was merely a recurring dream. On the third night, the officer, by now rather bored with all this psychic activity, told the ghost it would be impossible to get the Duke of Buckingham, one of the most important men in the kingdom, to listen to such nonsense. His reply would inevitably be 'Who told you this? A ghost; ah yes, I see – thank you. Have you been feeling quite well lately?'

But the determined ghost of Sir George would not give up. He insisted on telling the soldier some very private and personal information which only he and the duke could possibly know. At this the soldier was convinced, and set out at dawn to London to seek audience with the duke. He was shown in, and told of the ghostly visit of Sir George. Buckingham was unimpressed until the officer repeated the secret information which the ghost had imparted to him. The duke went as white as a sheet.

But it was too late for Buckingham to court the popularity he needed, and he was still the most hated man in England. He was murdered at Portsmouth in 1628 by an army officer, Lt John Felton, who became the people's hero overnight.

The plight of George III has recently been much publicised in a film, *The Madness of King George*, which has been successful on both sides of the Atlantic. George spent the last years of his long reign – he was king for 60 years, from 1760 to 1820 – locked up in his rooms at Windsor Castle, where he whiled away the hours by playing his harp. He was very lonely, and used to tap on the window to attract the attention of the sentries, or anyone else who was near. His ghost still does so today.

The afflicted monarch was nevertheless very popular during his reign, and was affectionately known as 'Farmer George', because of his interest in plants and agriculture. In 1811, his eldest son, also George, was appointed Prince Regent to rule on behalf of his father, who died in 1820.

One of the few amusements available to the lonely king was to watch the sentries as they paraded outside his window, and he was fond of waving and calling to them, and his ghost is still seen, smiling at his soldiers and cheering them on.

When he died, the old king lay in state in the chapel. The

guards still paraded under his windows over the North Terrace, and their commander was accustomed to the king's acknowledgement of his command 'eyes right'. George would always raise his right hand as he heard the order.

The day after the king died, the ceremony of the changing of the guard went on as usual. As the officer gave the order, he automatically looked out of the corner of his eye – and there was the royal figure he had seen so many times, right arm raised in salute. The young officer was William Knollys, of the famous Reading family. He went on to become an aide to the Prince of Wales, who as Edward VII, succeeded Queen Victoria to the throne in 1901.

There are many short and ephemeral tales told of sightings of ghosts by soldiers while on guard at the castle, but substantive evidence is sadly lacking. The brave military men would not deny their being partial to a tot or two, and endless hours on solitary duty at night have been known to play havoc with the imagination. Hence, the story of a sentry who claimed he saw the ghost of an elephant charging towards him on the East Terrace can be taken with a pinch of salt. The soldier reported that he fired at the animal, which promptly disappeared. The mark where his bullet hit the stonework is still there, despite his unlikely explanation.

Ghost stories abounded in Windsor town in days gone by, but the advent of the millenium seems to have discouraged their presence. The town and castle are now among the busiest tourist attractions in the world, with armies of local people toiling to keep the visitors supplied with food, drink, accommodation, and souvenirs. The spirits of the past seem largely to have faded away in the face of mounting commercialism and the huge crowds it brings. Ghosts seem to prefer the twilight world of uncertainty, where they are in command and can come and go as they please in terrifying splendour. Long crocodiles of tourists with instant cameras can't be very appealing to our illustrious ancestors. To put on a quick bit of manifestation just for their amusement would be far beneath their spectral dignity; a descent from the sublime to the ridiculous.

But in times gone by, the town was full of tales of witches and sorcery, as well as ghostly apparitions. The ghost of the physician who attended Charles II on his deathbed is reputed to ride through the town in a black carriage on the eve of a monarch's death. The doctor's ghostly journey starts from the site of a former inn, the Black Horse, and he wends his way the short distance to the castle to attend the dying king. The last recorded sighting of him was the day before Edward VII died in 1910.

The Nell Gwynne restaurant near to the castle gate was once the home of Charles II's illustrious mistress, and she lived there for some time. The famous orange seller's ghost is still sometimes heard on the premises.

In centuries gone by, fear of the unknown often caused severe reaction by ordinary people against anyone they suspected of having paranormal powers. Windsor was no exception, and in 1597 four old women of the town were tried and found guilty of witchcraft. They were executed at Abingdon, then the county town of Berkshire. The four women had lived peacefully at almshouses in Windsor until they fell victim to the accusation of sorcery, which was almost certainly untrue, and borne out of a malicious desire for revenge.

A stableman at a local inn was in the habit of giving a few coins to the old ladies in the almshouses. One morning he made such a donation to one of them, Elizabeth Rockingham.

She was a cantankerous old woman, and instead of thanking the man for his kindness, cursed him for giving her too little. Soon after, he fell ill with pains in his limbs, which was probably only rheumatism, but which he was convinced was the work of witchcraft. He was told he would be cured if he could draw the blood of the witch who had cast the spell, and the stableman decided to attack Elizabeth Rockingham, who he was convinced had cast the spell.

He scratched her until the blood flowed, and was promptly cured. Tongues began to wag, and the townspeople were soon saying that Mistress Elizabeth and her almshouse neighbours were witches. She was taken to Reading Gaol and 'encouraged to confess'. She soon implicated the other women, saying that all could transform themselves into animals, and that her neighbour kept a devil in the form of a toad. All of the women's pet cats were suddenly accused of being familiars with magic powers. Her inquisitors made her confess that her own familiar was a rat which sucked her blood.

Not surprisingly, Mistress Elizabeth fell ill in Reading Gaol, and accused her former friend and neighbour, Mother Duell, of taking away the use of her limbs so that her 'toes did rotte off her feete'.

It was a common test at this time to prick a 'witch's mark' – often just a mole – with a thorn. If it bled, the accused was condemned out of hand as a witch. Often the wounds turned septic, and it seems likely this is what happened to the unfortunate Elizabeth. She admitted causing the deaths of a local farmer and the town mayor by making an image of them with clay, and then sticking pins in it. This was something much feared by the frightened and ignorant populace, and the fate of the women was sealed; they and their pets, whom the women had admitted were devils in disguise, would have to be destroyed.

And so it was done, a not particularly remarkable event in an age when witch hunting was common, an age when superstition and dread of the unknown were much more powerful than reason and justice.

A Berkshire Medley of Unquiet Souls

BRACKNELL

UNDERNEATH the modern building of Bracknell College lies the site of the Hind's Head Inn. When it was built in the 15th century, it stood on isolated heathland and provided welcome refreshments for the travellers of the day. Dick Turpin is supposed to have frequented it for a while, and legend has it that there was a tunnel, large enough for a man on horseback, connecting the inn with the old manor house. When road works were being carried out in the 1960s, a large tunnel was found under what is now the roundabout by the Meteorological Office.

The inn had a macabre history, and many customers who stayed the night were never seen again, because the landlord had a nasty trick of getting them drunk and then murdering them for their money. Bracknell soon acquired a reputation for being an evil place, haunted by murdered spirits, and travellers would make a detour to avoid the town.

Bracknell's reputation was in some part restored when a traveller suspected the motives of the landlord at the Hind's Head and feigned drunkenness to see what was in store for hapless travellers. It soon became evident that they were thrown down a well and left to die. The landlord would assist them to a special bedroom, and then consign the inebriated guest down a secret trapdoor. On this occasion the man made good his escape and came back with the town watch. The landlord and his wife were hanged for murder.

Excavations in 1832 uncovered the well, which was full of human bones.

WOOLHAMPTON

The redoubtable Miss Emma Elizabeth Thoyts records the existence of a ghost at Douai Abbey over 100 years ago. Miss Thoyts lived at Sulhamstead and was the first woman in the world to write a military history book, *The History of the Berkshire Militia,* published in 1897.

Miss Thoyts' ghostly account tells of a young woman who died of unknown causes at the abbey school in about 1850, and was buried in the churchyard. Soon afterwards, a series of complaints were made by people who had slept in the room where the girl had died. All felt sure that someone entered the room, unseen and untouchable.

Miss Thoyts recorded 'The whole affair was discountenanced by Dr Crookall and the lady matron, Miss Edwards, who was a niece of Kemble, the actor. At length, a woman slept in the room, and in the morning, declared she had received a visit during the night.'

Miss Thoyts does not name the woman, but notes that she said to the matron 'I do hope that poor girl's face gets better, she looked so ill.' Miss Edwards was completely nonplussed, and asked the woman 'What girl?' The woman replied 'The poor thing that came to me last night with her face tied up – I suppose she could not sleep.'

Miss Edwards had some questions to ask, and the woman gave her an exact description of the young lady who had died in the room. The woman had never seen the girl, and had no knowledge that such a person had ever existed – or even of the rumour that the room was haunted. The woman thought one of the servants, suffering from some sort of illness, had accidentally wandered in, and had quickly departed on being challenged.

The incident was reported to the school authorities and prayers and masses were said for the unquiet spirit. Miss Thoyts concludes 'After that, no further visitations were ever heard of. The old college was pulled down in 1888, and the site ocupied by this particular room now forms part of the playground in front of the new college.'

SLOUGH

At Ditton Park, near Slough, a gardener found an old well and dug up some items dating from the 16th century near the ruins of an old chapel which had been sacked by soldiers of Henry VIII. The experience gave the gardener nightmares, and he told his employer he had dreamt of being at a funeral, with the metal coffin surmounted by a helmet and sword. There were soldiers there, dressed in the manner of Elizabethan times. He saw a priest in a red and white robe, who conducted a service in a language the gardener could not understand. The coffin was taken out and buried, still with sword and helmet on top.

The gardener awoke in a sweat as the soldiers turned to seize him to be buried with the coffin. Later, he recalled a group of monks dressed in black.

The gardener's employer noted that the man was an expert at water divining, was honest and reliable; and did not possess much of an imagination. He took his gardener to Windsor Castle, where he instantly recognised 16th century armour as being the type he had seen the soldiers wearing in his dream.

THATCHAM

The King's Head pub at Thatcham is reputed to be haunted by the ghost of a former landlady, Miss Fromont, who was the proprietor during the golden age of coaching in the 18th century. She grew wealthy on the proceeds of the traffic from London to Bath, and it seems she was unwilling to depart when called by her maker. Her ghost, wearing a grey silk dress, has been seen by past landlords and their families, walking gracefully through the upstairs rooms, and often through a wall just for good measure. Children have often been aware of her presence, which is usually not frightening. Local folklore suggests there was an establishment of medieval monks on the site in the middle ages, and that a tunnel links the pub with a secret escape route on the river

Kennet. Miss Fromont is remembered without ill will, and a street in the town is named after her.

BRIMPTON

Beware if you cross the bridge over the river at Brimpton on a dark winter's night. Legend has it that a group of young people were killed there many years ago, when their carriage overturned on the way to a hunt ball. The coach plunged into the river and they were all drowned.

On the anniversary of the tragedy, every January, phantom horses' hooves are heard, along with the rumble of wooden wheels with iron rims. When the phantom carriage reaches the bridge, there are the sounds of screaming as it sinks into the water, followed by deathly silence.

ETON

The Three Tuns pub which used to be in Eton High Street was haunted, according to a report in the local paper in 1979. The building had at some time been refurbished, and a woman customer saw the ghost of a man standing behind the landlord, at a point behind the bar where an old wall had been knocked down.

Landlord Bert Matthews was a former policeman and professional boxer, and although an unlikely candidate for psychic communication, he also had seen and heard the ghost, and had felt it brushing past him. Doors opened and closed on their own. The ghost was also seen by a woman cleaner.

ETON COLLEGE

A former Provost of Eton College, Dr M.R. James, was a celebrated writer of ghost stories in his time, the best known being *Ghost Stories of an Antiquary*, published in 1905, although it appears he did not address himself to Berkshire's ghosts.

The old college buildings have one or two spooks of their own, plus a rare case of a ghost being photographed.

Dr H.E. Luxmore, an Eton master in the 1920s, was very fond of his garden. After his death, a small pavilion to commemorate him was erected in the garden, and a couple of dozen of his friends attended a small ceremony. A photograph was taken to record the event, with all the dignitaries assembled in front of the camera. When the picture was developed, there to everyone's amazement was Dr Luxmore among his friends, an unmistakable figure with his flowing white hair and cape over his shoulders.

The college's most famous ghost is that of Jane Shore, one time mistress of Edward IV. In the 15th century, royal mistresses tended to enjoy lavish splendour whilst in favour, and abject misery when out of it. The discarded Jane found herself penniless and imprisoned, but was rescued when the Eton masters raised enough money to secure her release; which they were willing to do because Jane had managed to persuade her royal lover to desist from his intention of demolishing the college to spite the House of Lancaster, which had founded it.

The masters gave Jane a room in Lupton's Tower, facing the school yard, and she lived there for the rest of her life. She haunts the tower and adjoining cloisters, and is known as The Grey Lady.

During the blackout of World War Two, it was the custom of the police sergeant on night duty to call in at the Windsor and Eton waterworks. It was manned 24 hours a day, and the sergeant knew that if he called in at about midnight, the watchman would be brewing a cup of tea.

The watchman's hut was protected by a wall of sandbags, to reduce the effect of blast in case of bombing, but he could always hear the approach of the policeman, heralded by the crunch of his boots on the gravel, and the tick, tick, tick of the free-wheel of his bicycle.

It was just before midnight when the watchman put the kettle on. In the still of the night, he heard the familiar footsteps and the sound of the cycle. The reassuring noise drew steadily nearer, and then stopped. Puzzled, the watchman went outside. He could see no one. He waited for the sergeant to make his appearance. No one came, and by morning he was concerned for the sergeant's welfare.

Soon after sunrise, the daytime watchman came to relieve him, and the two discussed the uneventful night and the sergeant's failure to call in for his customary cup of tea. The night man told his relief that he had clearly heard the policeman approach and then suddenly vanish; what explanation could there be?

The man on the day shift had heard news that he reluctantly imparted to his night-time colleague. The sergeant had been killed the previous day. The night watchman had heard the footsteps of his phantom.

Index